four seasons

I dedicate *Four Seasons* to

my wonderful husband Uys –

without your encouragement and support

I would not have been able to write this book.

four seasons

Marita Pieterse

Photography Adriaan Vorster Styling Abigail Donnolly

First published in 2006 by Struik Publishers
(a division of New Holland Publishing
(South Africa) (Pty) Ltd)
New Holland Publishing is a member of
Johnnic Communications Ltd
Cornelis Struik House, 80 McKenzie Street,
Cape Town 8001
86–88 Edgware Road, London,
W2 2EA, United Kingdom
14 Aquatic Drive, Frenchs Forest,
NSW 2086, Australia
218 Lake Road, Northcote,
Auckland, New Zealand

www.struik.co.za

PUBLISHING MANAGER: Linda de Villiers
MANAGING EDITOR: Cecilia Barfield
EDITOR: Irma van Wyk
DESIGNER: Helen Henn
PHOTOGRAPHER: Adriaan Vorster
STYLIST: Abigail Donnolly
PROOFREADER and INDEXER: Joy Clack

Reproduction by Hirt & Carter Cape (Pty) Ltd
Printed and bound by Kyodo Printing Co
(Singapore) Pte Ltd

ISBN 1 77007 228 4 (9 781770 072282)

10 9 8 7 6 5 4 3 2 1

The authors and publishers would like to thank the following for the loan of their homeware products: Interior Trading, Plush Bazaar, Heartworks, Ethereal, Aldona Interiors, The Yellow Door

Acknowledgements

I am extremely grateful to –
My heavenly Father, the source of my inspiration and strength,
for giving me talents and abilities.
Struik Publishers, for giving me the opportunity to write this book.
Abigail Donnelly, for her stunning food styling.
My dear mom and dad, for their love and encouragement over the years.
My sister Elize and my friend Marianne, for helping with proofreading.
My friend Christel, for helping to test recipes.
Sandra Wolfaardt, from the Tshwane Market, for supplying information
about the seasonal availability of fruit and vegetables.
All my other friends and family, for their support and interest in this project.

Contact Marita at: info@kelkiewyn.co.za

contents

Introduction 7

Summer 10

Autumn 32

Winter 52

Spring 74

Special Occasions 98

Suggested Menus 126

Index 127

To everything there is a season …

Ecclesiastes 3:1

Introduction

This book is about the joy of seasonal cooking, of using fresh produce at its peak, simply prepared so as not to smother but rather complement it with whatever is added.

The book is also a celebration of the special charm of each season in this glorious country of ours, and a tribute to family and friends.

And lastly, this is a challenge to each and every one of you to get into the kitchen, to follow your instincts, be creative and have fun cooking.

A few basic guidelines

This book is not meant to be a guide to cooking, but a few things are so important for good results that I simply have to mention them. So here goes:

Read the recipe

Read through the entire recipe before you start cooking and make sure you have everything you need on hand. Be sure to read the cook's notes as well, as these often provide very useful information to ensure a good end result.

Cooking times and procedures

Keep in mind that cooking times are simply a guideline, as ovens and other factors vary. Do not mindlessly follow a recipe; cook with all your senses. *Look* at the colour of a pie crust to tell if it's been in the oven long enough, learn to *smell* when caramel is ready, *listen* if rice is cooking too vigorously, *taste* pasta to tell if it is cooked, *touch* bread dough to establish if it's been kneaded enough.

Browning meat or chicken

When browning meat or chicken, do it in batches or you will overcrowd the pan and the meat will stew rather than brown.

Herbs

Plant your own herb garden, even if it's just a few pots on the windowsill. There is hardly a recipe in this book that does not include some sort of herb, simply because I believe you cannot cook properly without fresh herbs. With the exception of oregano, which keeps its flavour quite well, dried herbs are just not the same.

If you have to use dried herbs, use half the quantity of fresh ones. Rather use Italian instead of ordinary (curly) parsley, especially in salads. Italian parsley is softer than the curly one and doesn't have to be chopped as finely.

If the recipe specifies 5 ml chopped herbs, chop the herbs first, and then measure them. If the recipe calls for 100 ml parsley leaves, chopped, measure them first and then chop.

Spices

Always buy spices in small quantities as they lose their flavour after a while. Store, tightly sealed, in a cool, dry place. Wherever possible, buy whole spices that can be dry-fried and ground before using. To dry-fry, place in a heavy-bottomed saucepan over medium heat, without any oil or butter, and stir with a wooden spoon until the spices become fragrant. Crush in a mortar or grind in a coffee grinder that you keep solely for this purpose. Buy nutmeg whole as well, and grate with a microplane grater, a nutmeg grater or the finest blade on an ordinary grater.

Nuts

Unless they are used in a cake mixture or something similar, it is usually better to roast nuts to bring out their flavour. This is especially important if you want to use them in salads or vegetable dishes. To do this, simply place in an ovenproof dish without any oil or butter, and roast at 200 °C for 8–10 minutes. Keep an eye on them so they don't burn, and stir once or twice in order to roast evenly. The roasting time will depend on the type and size of the nut, e.g. flaked almonds will roast more quickly than whole almonds. The time will also depend on the dish you use. The roasting time will be shorter if you use a metal roasting pan or baking sheet because metal is a better conductor of heat.

Seeds

Seeds, for instance sunflower and sesame, need to be toasted to bring out their flavour. This can be done in a dry frying pan over medium heat, as for the spices, or in the oven, as for the nuts.

Parmesan cheese

Always use freshly grated Parmesan cheese from Woolworths or cheese suppliers. The small packets purchased from supermarkets taste like cardboard or worse, and do not really contribute any taste to a dish. Keep grated Parmesan in the freezer to prevent it from going mouldy.

Sea salt

It may seem very 'cheffy' to cook with sea salt, but it is actually worth using something like Maldon® sea salt for sprinkling on roasted vegetables, in salads and salsas. However, it is not necessary to use it in cooking.

Olive oil

Use extra virgin only for salad dressings or when you want to add a bit of oil to a dish just before serving. Most of its flavour is lost when heated, so it's pointless cooking with it. Use virgin olive oil or plain olive oil for cooking. Keep all olive oils out of direct sunlight, stored in a cool, dry, dark place.

Stock

In an ideal world, we would all use home-made stock, which really is cheap to make and undoubtedly tastes better than cubes or stock powder. Unfortunately this is not always possible, so if you do use powdered stock, use about half the amount of powder specified on the container or the taste could be too salty or overpowering.

Eggs

All the recipes use large eggs.

Pastry

I prefer to make pastry in a food processor as it is very quick and easy to make, and prevents over handling. If you don't have a food processor, here's how you go about it, using any of the pastry recipes in this book (see pages 36, 48, 58, 70, 78, 114): Sift the flour, sugar (if called for in the recipe) and salt together in a mixing bowl. Rub in the butter until the mixture resembles fine breadcrumbs. Add the other ingredients, where applicable, e.g. grated Parmesan cheese or ground almonds (as specified in the recipe). Sprinkle most of the liquid specified in the recipe (egg or egg and water, whatever the case may be) over the dry ingredients and gently mix in with a fork until the pastry comes together. Add more liquid if it looks too dry but keep in mind that you may not need all of it. Chill the pastry.

Any pastry that has been chilled for more than an hour needs to stand at room temperature for about 10 minutes to soften slightly; otherwise it may crack when it is rolled out.

Roasted peppers

To roast peppers, cut them into quarters and remove and discard the seeds. Arrange in a single layer on a baking sheet, skin side up. Place under a preheated grill until the skins are blackened all over (move them around a bit during grilling to ensure even roasting). Immediately place in a plastic bag and twist to seal. Leave to cool for at least 15 minutes, then peel.

Store cupboard ingredients

This is a list of some basic dry ingredients that are handy to have around. I am not including obvious items like flour, sugar, vanilla essence, etc.

- brown or treacle sugar for baking, and to bring out the flavour of tomatoes
- canned tomatoes, preferably Italian
- canned tuna, for salads, pasta dishes and sandwiches
- castor sugar, for puddings, baking and meringues
- desiccated coconut, for puddings and baking
- condensed milk, for ice cream and sauces
- couscous, for making quick and interesting side dishes
- curry paste
- stock powder
- sweet chilli sauce
- dried bay leaves and oregano
- dried pasta
- golden syrup, for puddings and baking
- honey, for puddings, baking and marinades
- Maldon® sea salt, for sprinkling on salads and roasted vegetables
- mustard: Dijon, grainy and powder
- nuts, like pecans, almonds and pistachios; for salads, baking and desserts
- rice: basmati, jasmine, risotto and brown
- sunflower oil for frying
- olive oil for cooking and extra virgin olive oil for salad dressings
- olives
- peppadews™, for salads and sandwiches
- polenta or mealie meal
- seeds, like poppy and sesame, for sprinkling on food, and sunflower, for baking and adding to salads (store in the freezer)
- soy sauce, for adding flavour to sauces, stews and stir-fries
- spices: whole cumin, nutmeg and cinnamon; ground ginger, paprika and turmeric; crushed chilli; cayenne pepper; whole black peppercorns
- tomato paste, preferably Italian and in a tube
- vinegar: balsamic, red wine and white wine

Kitchen equipment

I am not a gadget fan, but some tools are really useful to have in the kitchen, sometimes producing a better result as well. A few items that will make your life in the kitchen easier are:

- a good set of knives – absolutely essential
- a potato ricer – for making the lightest, fluffiest mashed potato in a flash
- a microplane grater – for quick and easy grated lemon rind, chocolate, Parmesan cheese and nutmeg
- an electronic scale – essential for the accurate measuring of ingredients, especially when baking
- a food processor – for making pastry, pesto, breadcrumbs, etc.
- a liquidiser or hand-held blender – for soups, sauces and smoothies
- a mandolin (a grater with adjustable steel blades mounted on a plastic base) – useful for slicing or grating onions, cucumber and carrots

Life is just a bowl of cherries.

Lew Brown

Summer

fruit

apricots, bananas, blueberries, gooseberries, granadillas, grapes, litchis, mangoes, mulberries, nectarines, peaches, pineapples, plums, prickly pears, raspberries, rhubarb, spanspek (sweet melons), watermelons

vegetables

asparagus, aubergines, baby marrows, cabbages, chillies, cucumbers, lettuces, mealies, potatoes, red onions, tomatoes

Chilled Pea and Lettuce Soup
with Crispy Ham

Heat the oil in a frying pan over medium-low heat and fry the spring onions for about 5 minutes until soft but not brown. Add the potatoes and stir-fry for a few more minutes, then add the lettuce and stir until wilted. Pour in the stock and water. Bring to the boil and cook for about 15 minutes until the potatoes are tender. Add the peas and salt and pepper, and cook for 5 minutes more. Leave to cool a little, then liquidise the soup and place it in the fridge to cool down completely.

Meanwhile heat a non-stick frying pan and quickly fry the ham for about 2 minutes, until crisp. Remove from the pan and leave to cool, then crumble roughly.

Stir the yoghurt into the soup, check the consistency and add more stock or water if it is too thick. Taste the soup then add more salt and pepper if necessary. Spoon into serving dishes and sprinkle with the crumbled ham. Garnish with pea pods, if preferred.

cook's note: This soup needs plenty of salt and pepper to bring out the flavour, so make sure you season it well before serving.

advance preparation: The soup can be kept in the fridge for a day or two, or frozen, before adding the yoghurt. The ham can be fried a day in advance and stored in an airtight container.

30 ml olive oil
2 bunches spring onions, chopped
2 medium potatoes (±250 g), peeled and cubed
1 medium head of lettuce, leaves roughly torn
500 ml vegetable stock
500 ml water
500 g frozen peas
salt and pepper
40 g Black Forest or Parma ham
350 ml Greek yoghurt
pea pods to garnish (optional)

You will also need:
a liquidiser or hand-held blender

Serves 8

I know it sounds strange having lettuce in a soup but, trust me, it's delicious. Instead of liquidising it, the soup can be whizzed briefly in a food processor for a coarser texture. Serve the soup ice cold or at room temperature, with grissini (bread sticks).

Kofta Burgers
with Mango-Sweet Chilli Sauce

Place the beef, bread, onion, garlic, herbs, spices, salt and some freshly ground black pepper in a bowl, and mix together with your hands until well combined.

Divide the mixture into four and shape into patties. Preheat the grill or a griddle pan, or prepare the braai/barbecue. Brush the patties with olive oil, then grill or braai for about 12 minutes, turning occasionally, until the meat is browned all over and cooked through, but still juicy in the centre. Serve with the sauce.

Mango-sweet chilli sauce:
Mix the mango with the sweet chilli sauce. Taste, and add more chilli sauce if desired.

cook's note: If making the burgers in advance, it's better not to add salt to the mixture. Rather season the patties with salt just before cooking.

advance preparation: The minced meat mixture can be prepared a day in advance. Cover and refrigerate. The burgers can be shaped earlier in the day and refrigerated. The sauce can also be prepared a day in advance.

500 g minced beef
1 slice white bread, crusts removed, soaked in milk and squeezed dry
1 small onion, finely chopped
2 cloves garlic, crushed
50 ml chopped fresh mint or Italian parsley, or a combination of both
7.5 ml ground cumin
7.5 ml paprika
2.5 ml ground cinnamon
4 ml salt
freshly ground black pepper
olive oil, for brushing
salad leaves and toasted bread rolls, to serve (optional)

For the mango-sweet chilli sauce:
1 mango, peeled and cut into 1 cm pieces
±100 ml sweet chilli sauce

Serves 4

Koftas are spicy meatballs, very popular in North India. They are usually shaped around skewers and then cooked, but sometimes they can be a bit difficult to handle that way, so I have made them into patties. Serve the burgers with oven-baked potato wedges or store-bought kettle-fried chips.

Spice-rubbed Spatchcock Chicken

with Greek-style Salad

A spatchcock chicken is one that has been flattened, which ensures even and quicker cooking. To do this you will need a strong pair of kitchen scissors. With the parson's nose facing you, place the chicken on a chopping board, and cut each side of the parson's nose, taking out the middle bone. Turn the chicken over, open it out and press with the palm of your hand to crack the breastbone. Remove excess skin from the neck area.

Mix the spice rub, oil, garlic, lemon juice and rind together, and rub all over the chicken. Place the chicken in a plastic bag and refrigerate until needed.

Just before cooking, season the chicken with salt on all sides. Braai/barbecue over medium heat or cook in a Weber® for about 45 minutes until golden brown and cooked through.

When the chicken is almost done, brush the lemon slices with oil and braai until golden brown. Serve with the chicken.

Spice rub:
Mix everything together and store in an airtight container.

Salad:
Place the tomatoes, onion and parsley in a bowl and toss to mix. Arrange on a serving platter and scatter the feta and olives on top. Squeeze over a little lemon juice, drizzle with olive oil and season with salt and pepper. Serve at room temperature.

cook's note: To test if the chicken is cooked, pierce the thigh meat with a sharp knife. The juices should run clear.

It is essential to use Italian parsley, not ordinary (curly) parsley for the salad. If you cannot find it, replace the parsley with shredded basil or rocket.

To stone olives, place on a chopping board and bash with a large bladed knife.

advance preparation: The rub can be stored in an airtight container for a couple of weeks. The chicken can be rubbed and left overnight in the fridge, and can also be frozen after the rub has been applied. Defrost before cooking.

1 medium chicken, spatchcocked
30 ml spice rub (see below)
20 ml olive oil, plus extra for brushing the lemon slices
2 cloves garlic, crushed
10 ml lemon juice
finely grated rind of 1 lemon
salt
2 lemons, thickly sliced (optional)

For the spice rub:
30 ml dry-fried cumin seeds, crushed (see page 8)
20 ml dry-fried coriander seeds, crushed
30 ml dried oregano
20 ml sugar
15 ml dried rosemary, crushed
15 ml dried mint
10 ml paprika
5 ml coarsely ground black pepper
2.5 ml crushed chilli

For the salad:
±24 cherry tomatoes, halved
1 small red onion, halved and thinly sliced
200 ml roughly chopped fresh Italian parsley
125 g feta cheese, diced or crumbled
±20 Kalamata olives, stoned and halved
lemon juice
olive oil
sea salt and freshly ground black pepper

Serves 4

A rub is a dry alternative to a marinade, a quick way of adding flavour to meat, chicken, seafood or vegetables, and turning something plain into something special. Rubs have become quite trendy and you will find a wide variety in delis and most supermarkets. However, it is very easy to make your own rub for a fraction of the cost of the store-bought variety. A rub lasts for up to three months in an airtight container and makes a lovely hostess gift. In this recipe I add other ingredients to the rub in order to create a paste, but you can also just brush the chicken with olive oil and then press the rub onto it.

Cherry and Watercress Salad
with Warm Goat's Cheese

Brush the bread slices with olive oil and toast lightly on both sides under the grill. Cut the cheese into squares, about 3 cm thick; you need eight pieces of cheese altogether. Brush the pieces of cheese with oil on all sides and roll in the crushed almonds, coating them all over. Refrigerate until you are ready to serve the salad.

Place the watercress in a large mixing bowl with a little of the dressing and toss to coat. Add the cherries and mix gently. Divide between four serving plates.

Place the bread on a baking sheet and top each slice with a piece of almond-crusted cheese. Bake at 220 °C for about 5 minutes until the cheese starts to soften. Arrange two slices of bread on each plate of salad and serve immediately. Serve the rest of the dressing separately.

Dressing:
Whisk everything together.

cook's note: When buying cherries, look out for firm, glossy specimens without wrinkles, and always buy them with the stems on as this prevents them from rotting.

advance preparation: The dressing can be prepared a day in advance. The goat's cheese can be coated with almonds and refrigerated for up to 6 hours. Place on the bread just before baking.

8 slices French loaf
±30 ml olive oil
200 g goat's cheese
50 g flaked almonds, roasted and crushed
±500 ml (50 g) watercress
300 g fresh cherries

For the dressing:
30 ml olive oil
7.5 ml lemon juice
5 ml castor sugar
finely grated rind of 1 orange
salt and freshly ground black pepper

Serves 4 as a starter

This salad makes a very sophisticated starter, or it can be served as a light lunch, in which case the recipe will serve two people. For the cheese, use a block of semi-hard goat's cheese cut into squares; logs of soft goat's cheese are not really suitable for this dish.

Pork Fillet Kebabs

with Dried Apricot Couscous

60 ml olive oil
60 ml tomato sauce
30 ml honey
40 ml soy sauce
5 ml ground coriander
5 ml ground cumin
pinch of cayenne pepper
15 ml chopped fresh rosemary
750 g pork fillet, all fat and sinew removed and cut into 3 cm cubes

For the dried apricot couscous:

200 g (250 ml) couscous
250 ml hot chicken stock
30 ml olive oil
100 g soft dried apricots, thinly sliced
8–10 spring onions, thinly sliced (include some of the green parts)
70 g (125 ml) sunflower seeds, toasted
finely grated rind of 1 lemon
lemon juice to taste
salt and freshly ground black pepper

You will also need:

metal or wooden skewers

Serves 6

In a large glass bowl, mix together all the ingredients (except the pork). Add the pork and toss to coat. Place in the fridge to marinate for at least 2 hours or overnight.

Thread the marinated pork onto skewers. Char grill, grill or braai/barbecue over medium coals for about 20 minutes until cooked through. Serve with the dried apricot couscous and pita bread.

Dried apricot couscous:

Place the couscous in a large bowl. Combine the stock and oil, stir into the couscous and let it stand for about 10 minutes until the liquid has been absorbed. Fluff up the couscous with a fork and let it cool down. Stir in the apricots, spring onions, sunflower seeds and lemon rind. Add the lemon juice and season with salt and freshly ground black pepper.

advance preparation: The pork can be marinated a day in advance and can also be frozen in the marinade. Prepare the couscous a few hours in advance, but add the seeds shortly before serving so that they retain their crunch.

Couscous, the staple starch of North African cuisine, is ideal when you're in a hurry, as it needs no cooking. After soaking it in stock, it can be mixed with all sorts of ingredients, including chopped spring onions, tomatoes, roasted vegetables, herbs and spices. To complement the pork, I have combined the couscous with dried apricots. If you have fresh apricots, add some of these as well, but do include at least a few dried ones as they have a more intense flavour.

Rocket, Spanspek and Black Forest Ham Salad
with Mint Dressing

Heat a non-stick frying pan and quickly fry the ham for about 2 minutes until crisp. Drain on kitchen paper.

Place the rocket and spanspek in a large mixing bowl, add a small amount of dressing, just enough to coat the leaves, and toss lightly. Arrange on a serving platter and place the ham on top. Serve the rest of the dressing separately.

Dressing:
Whisk together the olive oil, lemon juice, sugar and mustard until well blended. Season with salt and pepper, and stir in the mint.

100 g Black Forest ham
±80 g rocket leaves, roughly torn if large
1 spanspek, peeled, seeded and cut into bite-size pieces

For the dressing:
75 ml olive oil
15 ml lemon juice
7.5 ml castor sugar
5 ml Dijon mustard
salt and freshly ground black pepper
30 ml finely chopped fresh mint

Serves 4 as a starter,
2 as a light lunch

This summery salad is very quick and easy to prepare. The combination of peppery rocket, sweet spanspek and salty ham is heavenly – perfect for a light lunch.

Mango Bread
with Crunchy Brown Sugar Topping

Halve about five of the pecan nuts and reserve for the topping; then roughly chop the rest. Peel the mangoes and cut 10 to 12 thin wedges from one of them by cutting with a sharp knife from the outside towards the pip. Set aside the halved pecans and mango wedges to use later for the topping. Finely dice or mash the rest of the mangoes and measure out 225 ml (250 g). Reserve the rest for another use.

Sift the flour, baking powder and salt together. Whisk the butter, castor sugar, eggs, lemon rind and vanilla essence until well blended, then stir in the 225 ml (250 g) diced or mashed mango. Fold the dry ingredients into the mango mixture and stir in the chopped pecan nuts.

Spoon the mixture into the prepared tin. Place a row of mango slices on top with the reserved pecan nuts here and there in between. Sprinkle with the brown sugar.

Bake at 180 °C for about 55 minutes until a skewer inserted into the centre comes out clean. Leave to cool in the tin for 10 minutes, then turn out onto a cooling rack. Leave to cool completely, then dust with icing sugar before cutting.

cook's note: Do not be concerned if the mixture looks curdled halfway through; all will be well in the end.

As with muffins, it is important not to over mix the batter, as this will make the bread leathery and dry.

advance preparation: The bread can be made at least two days in advance and can also be frozen.

75 g (150 ml) pecan nuts
3 ripe mangoes
180 g (325 ml) cake flour
10 ml baking powder
large pinch of salt
125 g (130 ml) butter, softened
175 g (225 ml) castor sugar
2 eggs
finely grated rind of 1 lemon
5 ml vanilla essence
50 ml brown sugar
icing sugar, for dusting

You will also need:
a 22 x 12 x 7 cm loaf tin, buttered and floured, and base-lined with non-stick baking paper

Makes 10 slices

My sister-in-law Tina was the inspiration for this recipe. Tina and her husband live on a smallholding near Tzaneen where they often have a surplus of mangoes in summer and do not know what to do with them. The bread can be served for tea, spread with butter; for brunch, toasted and drizzled with maple syrup; or for dessert, with vanilla ice cream and slices of caramelised mango, prepared in the same way as the caramelised nectarines (see page 125).

Mangoes freeze very well, so stock up while they are in season. To freeze, peel the mangoes, cut the flesh into chunks and place in the freezer in a suitable container. Once defrosted, the texture won't be quite the same as when fresh, but they are perfect for using in baking and for making mango curd or sauce.

Tabbouleh
with Preserved Lemon

100 g bulgur wheat
30 ml lemon juice
30 ml olive oil
½ preserved lemon (see page 34)
3 large tomatoes, seeded and cut into 1 cm pieces
6 spring onions, thinly sliced (include some of the green parts)
200 ml chopped fresh Italian parsley
100 ml chopped fresh mint
salt and freshly ground black pepper

Serves 4–6

Place the wheat in a fine sieve, rinse under cold water and drain well. Transfer to a large mixing bowl and stir in the lemon juice and oil. Leave to soak for 30 minutes.

Rinse the preserved lemon briefly in cold water to get rid of excess salt. Remove the flesh and discard. Dry the rind with kitchen paper and chop finely. Stir into the wheat, together with the rest of the ingredients and some salt and pepper. Mix well, taste, and adjust the seasoning if necessary.

cook's note: If you don't have preserved lemon, replace it with the grated rind of one large lemon.

advance preparation: The salad can be prepared a day in advance. Refrigerate in an airtight container.

Tabbouleh, a traditional Lebanese dish, is made from bulgur wheat, which has a nutty flavour and crunchy texture. Bulgur is available from supermarkets and health shops. Parsley is always used generously in this dish.

Brown and Wild Rice Salad
with Mango, Pecan Nuts and Mint

175 g (200 ml) brown and wild rice mix
4 ml salt
1.25 litres water
45 ml extra virgin olive oil
finely grated rind of 1 lemon
5 ml lemon juice
salt and freshly ground black pepper
4 or 5 sticks celery, thinly sliced
2 ripe but firm mangoes, cut into 1.5 cm pieces
75 g (150 ml) pecan nuts, toasted and roughly chopped
60 ml chopped fresh mint

Serves 6–8

Place the rice in a saucepan with the salt and water. Bring to boiling point and stir once. Turn down the heat, cover, and simmer gently for 35–40 minutes until the rice is cooked but still firm. Drain in a sieve, rinse under cold water and drain again thoroughly. Leave to cool.

Place the rice in a large mixing bowl and stir in the oil, lemon rind and lemon juice. Season with salt and pepper, and add the rest of the ingredients. Toss to combine, cover and refrigerate until needed. Serve at room temperature as an excellent side dish with roast chicken or fish.

advance preparation: The salad can be prepared a day in advance.

Mixed Pepper, Dried Fig and Pine Nut Salad

Place the salad leaves, peppers, feta cheese and figs in a large mixing bowl, add a little dressing and toss to coat. Arrange on a serving platter, scatter the pine nuts on top and garnish with the basil leaves. Serve the rest of the dressing separately.

Basil dressing:
Whisk together the oil and vinegar and season with salt and pepper. Stir in the shredded basil.

175 g mixed salad leaves
2 large peppers (red, orange or yellow), seeded and cut into thin strips
feta cheese (optional)
8 dried figs, thinly sliced
50 g (100 ml) pine nuts, toasted
fresh basil leaves, to garnish

For the basil dressing:
45 ml macadamia nut or olive oil
10 ml red wine vinegar
salt and freshly ground black pepper
8–10 fresh basil leaves, very finely shredded

Serves 6–8 as a starter or side dish

This is an unusual salad that is both delicious and nutritious. Use red peppers or a mixture of red, orange and yellow. Make sure that the peppers are very fresh and the dried figs soft and moist. Macadamia nut oil is now quite readily available and makes a great addition to a salad dressing. Replace with walnut or olive oil if you cannot find it.

Serve the salad as a starter, as a side dish with roast chicken or gammon; or add goat's or feta cheese and serve as a light lunch with crusty bread on the side.

Pecan Meringue Cake
with Mango and Granadilla Curd

Place the egg whites in a large bowl with a pinch of salt and whisk until stiff. Add 30 ml of the sugar, whisk again until stiff, then add the rest of the sugar bit by bit, whisking well after each addition. The mixture must be very stiff and glossy. Add the nuts and mix in well.

Divide the mixture between the prepared tins and bake at 180 °C for about 40 minutes until lightly browned and crisp on top. Turn the cakes out immediately, carefully peel off the paper and place on wire racks to cool.

Assembling the cake:
Whip the cream until stiff, then lightly fold in the mango and granadilla curd (do not whisk). Reserve a few tablespoons of the cream filling for the top, then sandwich the cakes with the rest of the filling. Pipe or spoon the reserved filling decoratively on the cake, arrange the pecan nuts on top and dust the cake with icing sugar.

cook's note: The nuts in the meringue make it soft and squidgy; so don't expect a hard meringue.

Do not be concerned if the cake cracks; this just adds to its charm.

advance preparation: The cakes can be baked two days in advance. Store in an airtight container. Once filled, the cake is best eaten on the same day.

For the cake:
6 egg whites
pinch of salt
300 g (375 ml) castor sugar
150 g (300 ml) pecan nuts, roasted and roughly chopped

To assemble the cake:
150 ml cream, chilled
150 ml mango and granadilla curd (see page 30)
few roasted pecan nuts
icing sugar, for dusting

You will also need:
2 x 23 cm springform tins, lined with foil and sprayed with non-stick cooking spray

Serves 8

This recipe is based on a recipe from Leith's cookery school in London. During my training there, we had to bake this cake for one of our practical exams. Upon returning to South Africa everyone who tasted the cake loved it, and I ended up baking one after the other for family, friends and the functions I catered for. Eventually I got so sick and tired of it I completely stopped baking it. In fact, I had actually forgotten all about it until somebody recently mentioned it again, commenting on how good it was. So here is the famous cake, with a bit of a face-lift. And it is still delicious.

Apricots in Rosemary Syrup
with Pistachio Nuts and Greek Yoghurt

60 g (75 ml) sugar
75 ml water
15 ml honey
finely grated rind of 1 lemon
20 cm sprig of fresh rosemary, plus extra for garnishing
8 fresh apricots, quartered
±25 g pistachio nuts, roasted
Greek yoghurt, to serve

Serves 4–6

Place the sugar, water, honey, lemon rind and rosemary in a small saucepan over low heat, and stir until the sugar dissolves. Simmer for 5 minutes, adding the apricots for the last minute. Remove from the heat, cover and leave to cool.

Remove the rosemary and serve the apricots with a few nuts sprinkled on top and a good dollop of yoghurt. Garnish with the extra rosemary.

cook's note: If the apricots are under ripe, double the amount of sugar and water in the recipe and poach them for about 10 minutes in the sugar syrup to bring out their flavour. Remove the apricots and reduce the sauce until syrupy.

This simple, refreshing dish is lovely for brunch, served with Greek yoghurt, or for dessert, teamed with slices of mango bread (see page 22) and vanilla ice cream. The pistachio nuts can be replaced with flaked or slivered almonds or sunflower seeds.

Catalan Cream
with Mango and Litchi Compote

Dissolve the cornflour in a few tablespoons of the milk. Place the rest of the milk, the cream and lemon rind in a saucepan. Place over medium heat, bring to the boil, then remove from the heat.

Whisk together the egg yolks and sugar until pale, then whisk in the cornflour mixture. Pour some of the warm cream mixture onto the egg yolk mixture and mix well. Whisk in the rest of the cream mixture until smooth.

Pour the mixture into a clean saucepan, place over lowish heat and stir constantly with a wooden spoon for about 10 minutes until the mixture thickens enough to leave a clear trail when a finger is drawn across the back of the spoon. Remove from the heat and leave to cool for about 15 minutes, stirring occasionally to avoid a skin forming.

Divide evenly among the dishes and refrigerate for a few hours or overnight.

Dust the catalan creams generously with icing sugar and, using a small blowtorch, glaze them until they become a rich golden brown colour. Repeat this three times for a good, crisp topping. Alternatively, place under a preheated grill to caramelise the sugar. Refrigerate for at least 15 minutes or up to 3 hours. Serve with the mango and litchi compote.

Mango and litchi compote:
Mix the mango and litchis together. Spoon on top of the catalan creams and sprinkle with lavender flowers.

cook's note: Do not be concerned if a skin forms on the surface of the custard; the skin will protect the custard from the heat while the sugar is being caramelised.

advance preparation: The catalan creams can be prepared a day in advance, without caramelising the top, which should only be done a couple of hours before serving.

15 ml cornflour
150 ml milk
400 ml cream
finely grated rind of 1 lemon
6 egg yolks
90 g (115 ml) sugar
icing sugar, for grilling

For the mango and litchi compote:
1 small mango, peeled and diced
12–15 litchis, peeled, pitted and diced
fresh lavender flowers, to decorate (optional)

You will also need:
6 x 8.5 cm ramekins or other flameproof dishes with a capacity of 150 ml

Serves 6

Similar to crème brûlée and just as delicious, catalan cream hails from the Catalonia region in Spain. The clever preparation method eliminates the need for baking in a bain-marie *as many recipes for crème brûlée do, while the cornflour helps to quickly thicken the mixture without the danger of curdling.*

Mango and Granadilla
Queen of Puddings

Place the cream, milk and castor sugar in a small saucepan, and stir over low heat until the sugar has dissolved. Add the butter and stir until melted. Remove from the heat and stir in the rind and breadcrumbs. Leave to stand for 10 minutes, then whisk in the egg yolks. Pour into the dishes and bake at 180 °C for about 20 minutes until set.

Let them cool down for 15 minutes, then spread the curd over the breadcrumb bases, dividing equally.

Meringue topping:
To make the topping, place the egg whites in a large bowl with a pinch of salt. Using an electric whisk and clean beaters, whisk the egg whites until stiff but not dry. Add 30 ml of the castor sugar and whisk again until stiff. Gradually whisk in the remaining castor sugar and beat until thick and glossy.

Spoon the meringue over the curd, piling it up high. Sprinkle a tiny bit of sugar over each pudding and bake for about 7 minutes at 220 °C until golden brown.

Mango and granadilla curd:
Halve the granadillas, scoop out the flesh and place in a sieve set over a bowl. Press with the back of a spoon to extract the juice. Measure the juice and, if necessary, add lemon juice to make up 100 ml. Put the juice and the rest of the ingredients in a saucepan and cook over medium-low heat, stirring continuously, until the mixture thickens and has the consistency of thick cream. Pour through a sieve into a bowl and let it cool down. Refrigerate or freeze until required.

advance preparation: The curd will keep for a week or two in the fridge and can also be frozen. The breadcrumb base for the puddings can be baked a couple of hours in advance. Spoon the curd over, make the meringue topping and bake shortly before serving.

300 ml cream
300 ml milk
50 g (60 ml) castor sugar
50 g (50 ml) butter
finely grated rind of 1 lemon
100 g fresh white breadcrumbs (about 4 slices)
4 eggs, separated
400 ml mango and granadilla curd (see recipe below)

For the meringue topping:
pinch of salt
60 g (75 ml) castor sugar, plus about 5 ml to sprinkle on top

For the mango and granadilla curd (makes about 600 ml):
6 large granadillas
lemon juice, if necessary
1 large mango, liquidised (you need 250 ml purée)
85 g (90 ml) butter, cut into 1.5 cm pieces
125 g (150 ml) sugar
4 egg yolks and 1 whole egg
grated rind of 1 lemon

You will also need:
6 x 250 ml ovenproof dishes, buttered and placed on a rimmed baking sheet

Serves 6

I know it's summer and you're not supposed to serve warm puddings, but this one is really light, so you can get away with it. Furthermore, once you've tasted it, you'll want to make it again in winter, so now is the time to freeze mangoes and granadillas for future use. Queen of Puddings is a classic English pudding usually made with jam or marmalade, sometimes with lemon curd, with a fluffy meringue topping. My version is made with mango and granadilla curd. The tanginess of the curd works very well with the sweetness of the pudding. Apart from making the curd, it is very quick and easy to put together, using store cupboard ingredients. The curd is delicious as a topping for scones, a filling for meringue nests or small tartlet cases. Serve the puddings warm, fresh from the oven, but not piping hot.

No spring nor summer beauty hath such grace,
As I have seen in one autumnal face.

John Donne

Autumn

fruit

apples, avocados, gooseberries, granadillas, grapefruit, grapes, lemons, oranges, pears, plums

vegetables

beetroot, butternut, cauliflower, chillies, green beans, leeks, mushrooms, patty pans, spinach, sweet peppers, sweet potatoes

Preserved Lemons

Place about two tablespoons of salt in the bottom of each jar. Holding a lemon upright, cut it into quarters, ending just before the base, so that you have four quarters attached at the stem. Carefully open up the lemon and place about a tablespoonful of coarse salt inside, then close it up again and place it in the jar. Repeat with more lemons, packing them in tightly. Sprinkle over a few more tablespoonfuls of salt, add the lemon juice to cover, close tightly and refrigerate for at least a month before using, occasionally turning the jar.

Before using, rinse the lemon to get rid of excess salt, remove and discard the flesh, and cut the skin into strips or dice.

advance preparation: It is essential to make the lemons a month in advance. They keep (almost) forever in the fridge.

lots of coarse salt
lemons, as many as you wish, well washed
fresh lemon juice

You will also need:
sterilised glass jars

Preserved lemons have always been used in Moroccan cooking but are now also used in other cuisines. More mellow than fresh lemons, their aroma enhances salads (see page 23), salad dressings, marinades, stews, fish and chicken dishes (see page 45).

Pan-fried Mozzarella and Salami Sandwiches

Place four slices of bread on a work surface and cover them with the sliced mozzarella, dividing it equally. Season the cheese lightly with salt and pepper. Divide the salami, peppadews™ and parsley among the four slices of bread, then cover with the remaining slices of bread.

Whisk the eggs and milk together and season with salt and pepper. Heat the oil in a large frying pan over medium heat. Carefully and briefly dip the sandwiches in the egg mixture, covering them all over and pressing the edges to seal. Working in batches and pressing them down with an egg lifter, fry the sandwiches for 3–5 minutes on each side until golden brown and the cheese starts melting.

advance preparation: The cheese, salami, parsley and peppers can all be prepared the night before. Store in plastic bags in the fridge.

8 slices white bread
200 g mozzarella cheese, thinly sliced
salt and freshly ground black pepper
60 g salami (about 5 slices), cut into thin strips
6–8 peppadews™, thinly sliced
100 ml roughly chopped fresh Italian parsley
3 eggs, lightly beaten
50 ml milk
±50 ml sunflower or olive oil

Serves 4

Serve for a special breakfast, for lunch or as a light supper with a salad.

Pizza

with Crisp Smoked Ham and Avocado

For the pizza dough:
250 g (450 ml) bread flour
5 ml instant dried yeast
2.5 ml salt
30 ml olive oil
±175 ml lukewarm water

For the topping:
175 g mozzarella cheese, coarsely grated
5 ml dried oregano
freshly ground black pepper
50 g shaved smoked ham, roughly torn
±15 ml olive oil
1 or 2 ripe avocados, sliced and brushed with lemon juice
salt and freshly ground black pepper

You will also need:
a large baking sheet, lightly greased with oil or sprayed with non-stick cooking spray

Makes 1 large pizza

Mix the flour, yeast and salt together in a large mixing bowl. Pour in the olive oil and most of the water. Mix with a wooden spoon, adding more water if necessary to form a soft dough. Turn out onto a lightly floured work surface and knead for about 10 minutes until smooth and elastic (this can also be done in an electric mixer, using the dough hook). Place the dough in a clean bowl, cover with a damp tea towel and leave to rise for about 1½ hours until doubled in size.

Knock back the dough by placing it on a lightly floured surface and kneading it for a minute or two to knock out the air. Roll the dough out very thinly into a circle roughly 35 cm in diameter and place on the prepared baking sheet.

Topping:
Spread the mozzarella over the pizza base, then sprinkle with the oregano and black pepper. Arrange the ham on top and bake for about 10 minutes at 230 °C until golden brown and crisp.

As soon as the pizza comes out of the oven, drizzle over the olive oil. Season the avocado with salt and pepper and arrange on the pizza.

cook's note: To ensure an authentic crisp crust, place a large unglazed quarry tile on the bottom shelf of your oven. Preheat the oven with the tile in for at least 20 minutes before baking the pizza. Place the pizza directly on the tile, or first on a greased baking sheet or a greased sheet of heavy-weight foil and then on the heated tile.

advance preparation: After knocking it back, the dough can be refrigerated for up to a day and can also be frozen.

When it comes to pizza, people can usually be divided into two camps: some like their pizza thin and crispy while others prefer theirs thick and juicy. Personally, I want to be able to pick up a slice and eat it by hand. That is why mine leans more towards authentic Italian-style pizza, where the crust is not drenched with cheese and toppings, as you often find in popular restaurants in our country. However, if that's the way you prefer your pizza, feel free to increase the quantities of cheese and ham. Be sure to use wafer-thin ham, which becomes nice and crispy in the oven. If you don't want to make the dough yourself, buy it ready-made from a supermarket.

Roasted Pepper, Olive and Feta Tartlets

For the pastry:
200 g (365 ml) cake flour
large pinch of salt
120 g butter (125 ml), cut into 1.5 cm cubes and chilled
30 ml freshly grated Parmesan cheese
1 egg, lightly beaten with 30 ml water

For the filling:
3 large peppers, red and yellow, roasted and peeled (see page 9)
16 black olives, stoned
100 g feta cheese, crumbled
10–12 fresh basil leaves, shredded, plus a few extra for garnishing
160 ml cream
2 eggs
salt and freshly ground black pepper
5 ml chopped fresh thyme
5 ml chopped fresh rosemary
35 g (45 ml) freshly grated Parmesan cheese

You will also need:
6 x 10 cm metal tart tins, preferably loose-bottomed ones

Makes 6 x 10 cm tartlets

Place the flour and salt in a food processor and pulse to blend. Add the butter and Parmesan cheese, and process until the mixture resembles fine breadcrumbs.

With the motor running, start adding the egg mixture and process just until the dough comes together (you may not need all of the liquid). Form the dough into a log, about 7 cm in diameter, place in a plastic bag and refrigerate for at least 30 minutes, or freeze for 15 minutes.

Place the pastry log on a lightly floured work surface and cut into six rounds. Roll out each round until about 4 mm thick and large enough to fit the tin. Line the tins with pastry and cut off the excess. Refrigerate for at least 30 minutes, or freeze for 15 minutes.

Prick the pastry cases lightly with a fork and line with foil or non-stick baking paper. Fill with dried beans and bake at 190 °C for 12 minutes. Remove the beans and paper and bake for about 6 minutes more until the crust is baked through and beginning to brown.

Filling:
Cut a quarter red and a quarter yellow pepper into thin strips and set aside, then roughly chop the rest of the peppers. Halve a few of the olives and set aside. Roughly chop the rest.

Divide the feta between the pastry cases, followed by the chopped peppers, chopped olives and the shredded basil. Whisk the cream and eggs together, season the mixture with salt and pepper, and stir in the chopped thyme and rosemary. Pour into the tartlet cases, arrange the reserved peppers and olives on top, and sprinkle over about half of the Parmesan. Bake at 180 °C for about 20 minutes until golden brown and puffed, and all but the very centre is set. Remove from the oven and sprinkle over the remaining Parmesan. Garnish with the extra basil leaves.

cook's note: Never overwork pastry or add too much water to it; this will make it tough.

The secret to a creamy, moist tartlet is to take it out of the oven before the very centre is set. After being removed from the oven the tartlets continue cooking for a few minutes, which means that they will be dry if you leave them in the oven until set all the way through.

advance preparation: Pastry keeps for a few days in the fridge and can also be frozen. The baked cases will keep for a couple of days in an airtight container. The baked tartlets are best eaten on the day they are made, but they can be reheated at 180 °C for about 10 minutes.

The tartlets can be served as a starter or as a light lunch with salad. You can also cut them into quarters and serve as a snack. The herbs can be varied according to what is available, but do try to include basil and rosemary for a real Mediterranean flavour.

Cheesy Ham and Potato Cakes
with Avocado

Boil the potatoes in their skins until tender, drain well, then briefly return to the heat to dry out well. Peel and mash while still warm. Stir in the egg, flour, salt, cheese, ham, chives, and some pepper.

Divide the mixture into eight and form into cakes. Place about 50 ml oil in a large frying pan over medium heat. As soon as the oil is hot, add four of the cakes and flatten them slightly with an egg lifter. Fry the cakes until golden brown, about 5 minutes on each side, adding more oil if necessary. Place on a baking sheet in the oven to keep warm and fry the rest of the cakes.

Arrange a few salad leaves on four serving plates and place two potato cakes on each plate. Place a slice or two of avocado on each potato cake, garnish with extra chives and serve immediately.

cook's note: The potatoes must be really dry before you mash them. If necessary, dry them with kitchen paper after draining.

If you are using leftover mashed potato, you will need about 400 g.

advance preparation: As with most food, the cakes are at their best when freshly made, but they can be reheated by placing them on a baking sheet in a 180 °C oven for about 10 minutes.

This is a quick and easy midweek supper and a clever way of using leftover mashed potato. Serve with a tomato salad and crusty bread. The cakes can be prepared in advance, making them ideal for brunch or breakfast too, perhaps topped with a poached egg.

500 g potatoes
1 egg, lightly beaten
35 g (60 ml) cake flour
2.5 ml salt
50 g mature Cheddar cheese, finely grated
80 g smoked ham, cut into strips
50 ml snipped chives, plus extra for garnishing
freshly ground black pepper
±75 ml sunflower oil
handful of salad leaves of your choice
1 or 2 avocados, sliced

Serves 4

Spaghetti Carbonara
with Rocket

2 eggs
1 egg yolk
50 ml full-cream milk
35 g (45 ml) freshly grated Parmesan cheese, plus extra for serving
salt and freshly ground black pepper
200 g spaghetti
15 ml olive oil
75 g Black Forest ham, cut into thin strips
large handful of rocket, roughly chopped

Serves 2

In a large mixing bowl, whisk together the eggs, egg yolk, milk and Parmesan cheese. Season the mixture with salt and pepper.

Cook the spaghetti according to the instructions on the packet until *al dente*.

While the spaghetti is cooking, heat the oil in a large frying pan. Add the ham and fry for about 2 minutes until crisp. Remove the ham from the pan and set aside. Keep the pan warm over low heat.

Drain the spaghetti quickly, transfer it to the warm pan and immediately pour over the egg mixture. Toss to combine (the heat of the pasta will cook the egg). Stir in the ham and the rocket and serve with extra Parmesan.

Carbonara is a traditional Italian dish of pasta with bacon and egg. For my version I use Black Forest ham instead of bacon, and I add some rocket for a bit of extra colour. You can replace the ham with bacon if you prefer. Pasta should always be cooked al dente, *which means 'to the tooth', implying that it should be cooked through but still firm to the bite. Make sure you have all the ingredients ready in advance so that you can work quickly once the pasta is cooked.*

Mushroom Ragout
with Crisp Polenta Wedges

Melt the butter in a large frying pan, add the onion and cook for about 10 minutes until soft. Remove from the pan and set aside.

Add 15 ml oil to the pan, turn up the heat, add half of the mushrooms, together with some salt and freshly ground black pepper, and fry over high heat for 2–3 minutes until lightly browned. Repeat with the remaining mushrooms, adding more oil if necessary.

Return all the mushrooms and the onion to the pan over low heat. Add the flour and stir until well incorporated, then add the stock, milk, tomato paste and soy sauce, and stir until smooth. Simmer for about 5 minutes until thickened. Stir in the nutmeg and parsley. Add more stock if it looks dry. Serve with the polenta wedges.

Polenta wedges:
Bring the stock to the boil in a large saucepan. Add the polenta in a steady stream, whisking or stirring constantly with a wooden spoon. When all the polenta has been added, cover the saucepan, turn down the heat and simmer for about 20 minutes, stirring regularly, until the mixture comes away from the side of the pan. Stir in the butter, thyme, about two-thirds of the Parmesan, and salt and pepper to taste. Pour into the prepared Swiss roll tin and spread out evenly, about 1.5 cm thick. Leave to cool, then cut into triangles.

Arrange the triangles on the prepared baking sheet, brush with olive oil and sprinkle with the remaining Parmesan. Bake at 200 °C for about 15 minutes until heated through. If desired, place under a preheated grill to brown the cheese.

advance preparation: The ragout can be made a day in advance. Refrigerate and reheat over low heat. The polenta can be cooked and poured into the baking tray a day in advance. Cover and refrigerate.

30 g (30 ml) butter
1 large onion, thinly sliced
±30 ml olive oil
400 g mushrooms, sliced
salt and freshly ground black pepper
20 ml cake flour
±200 ml chicken or vegetable stock
100 ml milk
10 ml tomato paste
5 ml soy sauce
1.25 ml freshly grated nutmeg
75 ml chopped fresh Italian parsley

For the polenta wedges:
750 ml vegetable stock
145 g (200 ml) polenta
30 g (30 ml) butter
15 ml fresh thyme leaves
60 g (75 ml) freshly grated Parmesan cheese
salt and freshly ground black pepper
±45 ml olive oil

You will also need:
a Swiss roll tin, brushed with oil
a baking sheet, brushed with oil

Serves 4

In this recipe the ragout is teamed with polenta wedges, a great main course for vegetarians. The ragout can also be served as a side dish with meat or chicken, stirred into cooked pasta, as a filling for pancakes or as a topping for baked potatoes, rice or polenta. Try to use portabellini mushrooms, which have a better flavour than white button mushrooms. Also try using tomato paste in a tube for better flavour and easier storage.

Pork Fillet
with Caramelised Onions and Plums

Heat about 30 ml oil in a large frying pan, add the onions and cook for about 10 minutes until soft. Stir in half of the brown sugar, turn up the heat and fry the onions for about 3 minutes until caramelised. Remove the onions from the pan and set aside.

Dip the pork in the seasoned flour and shake off the excess. Add another 15 ml oil and half of the butter to the pan. When the butter has melted, fry the pork over medium-high heat until golden brown on both sides. Remove from the pan and set aside.

Deglaze the pan with the verjuice or wine, then stir in the stock and rosemary. Return the pork to the pan and simmer gently for 10–15 minutes until cooked through. Stir in the onions, taste and add more salt and pepper if necessary. Keep warm over low heat.

Melt the remaining butter in another frying pan. When the butter starts foaming, add the plums and sprinkle over the remaining brown sugar. Turn up the heat to medium-high and fry the plums for about 5 minutes until golden brown on both sides. Transfer the pork to a serving dish, scatter the plums over and garnish with sprigs of rosemary.

cook's note: To deglaze a pan means to loosen the flavourful sediment stuck to the bottom of the pan by adding liquid and stirring it while it boils. The liquid can be stock, water, wine or even fruit juice, whatever is appropriate.

±45 ml olive oil
2 large onions, thinly sliced
40 g (45 ml) brown sugar
800 g pork fillet, trimmed and cut into 2 cm thick slices
±100 g (±175 ml) cake flour, seasoned with salt and freshly ground black pepper
45 g (45 ml) butter
60 ml verjuice or dry white wine
400 ml chicken stock
15 ml chopped fresh rosemary, plus a few sprigs for garnishing
4 ripe but firm plums, cut into 2 cm thick wedges

Serves 4–6

Verjuice, which means green juice, is the unfermented juice of unripe wine grapes. Its slight sweetness and mild acidity make it ideal for salad dressings, for giving a sauce a more piquant taste in place of vinegar or lemon juice, or for deglazing a saucepan, as in this recipe. It is available at most supermarkets and keeps very well in the fridge. The downside is that it is rather expensive, so if you do not plan on using it often, simply use dry white wine for this recipe, as indicated. Serve the pork with couscous and nuts or crisp potato wedges.

Creamy Chicken and Leek Pie
with Polenta Crust

Heat the butter and 15 ml oil in a large frying pan over medium-low heat. Cook the leeks for about 10 minutes until soft but not browned. Remove from the pan and set aside.

Season the chicken lightly with salt and pepper. Add more oil to the pan, add the chicken and stir-fry over fairly high heat for 5–6 minutes until well browned on all sides. Return the leeks to the pan and stir in the paprika and crème fraîche or sour cream (do not let it boil). Taste, and add more salt and pepper if necessary.

Transfer the chicken to the prepared dish, spoon over the polenta crust and arrange the pepper strips in a lattice fashion on top. Bake at 200 °C for 25–30 minutes until the crust is golden brown and cooked through.

Polenta crust:
Mix the flour, polenta, baking powder, paprika and salt together in a mixing bowl. Whisk the egg, milk and oil together lightly, pour into the dry ingredients and mix well with a fork to form a smooth batter.

cook's note: Crème fraîche, an important ingredient in French cooking, is cream that has been treated with a culture to give it a light acidity without sourness. It lasts longer in the fridge than cream, which is useful when half a tub is required and the rest kept for later use. Another advantage is that it doesn't curdle when heated, making it ideal for sauces. Make your own by mixing equal quantities of cream and buttermilk. Leave it, covered, at room temperature for 12 hours or until set. Store in the fridge where it should last for about a week.

Wash leeks well as there is often sand between the layers.

Do not cook the chicken too long at browning stage or it will be overcooked after the additional cooking time in the oven.

advance preparation: Cook the chicken and leeks in advance, then refrigerate. Reheat briefly the next day, stir in the crème fraîche or sour cream and paprika, and continue with the recipe. The pepper can be roasted and peeled a day in advance. Keep in a plastic bag in the fridge.

30 g (30 ml) butter
±30 ml olive oil
300 g leeks (about 4 large ones), sliced
4 chicken breasts (about 400 g), skinless and deboned, cut into large bite-size pieces
salt and freshly ground black pepper
5 ml paprika
150 ml crème fraîche or sour cream
1 red pepper, roasted, peeled and cut into strips (see page 9)

For the polenta crust:
100 g cake flour
60 g (85 ml) polenta
10 ml baking powder
2.5 ml paprika
2.5 ml salt
1 egg
125 ml milk
75 ml sunflower oil

You will also need:
a greased ovenproof dish, roughly 23 x 18 cm in size

Serves 4

This dish is unbelievably quick and simple and the red pepper lattice topping looks very appealing.

Moroccan-style Chicken Phyllo Pie

±60 ml olive oil
1 bunch spring onions, chopped (include some of the green parts)
1 large clove garlic, crushed
5 ml ground cumin
2.5 ml paprika
8 chicken breasts (±700 g), skinless and deboned, cut into large bite-size pieces
salt and freshly ground black pepper
10 ml cake flour
100 ml chicken stock
½ preserved lemon, thinly sliced
50 g (about 8) green olives, stoned and thinly sliced (optional)
100 ml chopped fresh coriander
5 or 6 sheets phyllo pastry
melted butter
sesame seeds, preferably black

You will also need:
a 24 cm loose-bottomed tin, brushed with butter

Serves 6–8

Surprisingly easy to make, this pie is a good choice for entertaining as the filling can be made a day in advance. If you don't want to bother with the phyllo pastry, the chicken can be served with couscous or rice. The recipe calls for preserved lemon, which is also a breeze to make (see page 34), but until yours is ready for use, replace it with the grated rind of one large lemon. Bear in mind that the flavour is not quite the same.

Heat 30 ml olive oil in a large frying pan and cook the spring onions for about 10 minutes until softened. Add the garlic, cumin and paprika, stir for a minute or two, then remove the onion mixture from the pan and set aside.

Lightly season the chicken with salt and pepper. Heat more oil in the pan and, working in batches, fry the chicken over high heat, about 4 minutes per batch, until nicely browned.

Return all the chicken and the onion mixture to the pan, and stir in the flour. Add the chicken stock, bring to the boil and simmer for about 2 minutes until thickened. Remove from the heat and stir in the lemon, olives and coriander. Taste and adjust the seasoning. Leave to cool.

Brush one sheet of phyllo pastry with butter and place in the prepared tin, allowing it to hang over the edges. Brush another sheet with butter and place at an angle over the first sheet. Repeat with two more sheets of pastry.

Spoon the chicken mixture into the phyllo-lined tin, spreading it out evenly. Bring the overhanging sheets of phyllo in over the filling. Brush another sheet of pastry with butter, crumple it and place it on top of the filling to form a lid. If necessary, repeat with another sheet to ensure that the filling is completely covered with pastry. Brush the pastry with more butter and sprinkle with sesame seeds. Bake at 200 °C for about 20 minutes until golden brown. Remove the pie from the tin, cut into wedges with a serrated knife and serve immediately.

cook's note: Do not cook the chicken too long at browning stage or it will be overcooked after the additional cooking time in the oven.

To prevent the phyllo pastry from drying out, brush one sheet at a time with butter. Keep the others covered by placing the thin sheet of plastic the pastry comes wrapped in on the stack of pastry sheets, with a damp tea towel on top.

Black sesame seeds are available from Chinese supermarkets.

advance preparation: The chicken filling can be prepared a day in advance and refrigerated. Bring to room temperature before using.

Pear and Pecan Nut Cake
with Cream Cheese Frosting

Sift together the flour, bicarbonate of soda, salt, cinnamon and ginger. Using an electric whisk, beat the sugar, eggs, oil and vanilla for about 5 minutes until well blended. Stir the dry ingredients into the egg mixture and mix until fully incorporated. Add the pecan nuts, coconut and grated pear, and mix in well. Spoon into the prepared tins and bake at 180 °C for 45–50 minutes until the cakes are firm to the touch and a tester comes out clean. Let the cakes cool down in the tin for about 30 minutes. Turn out the cakes, remove the baking paper and place on a wire rack to cool completely.

Frosting:
Beat the cream cheese and butter together until smooth. Add the icing sugar and beat again until well mixed. Use half of the mixture to sandwich the cakes together and spread the other half on the top. Sprinkle with cinnamon and decorate with dried pear slices, if desired.

cook's note: To make the dried pear slices, slice a whole, unpeeled pear into very thin slices. Spread out on a baking sheet lined with non-stick baking paper, sprinkle with icing sugar and dry out in the oven at 100 °C for about 2 hours until crisp.

The cake is delicious as a dessert as well. Bake it in a large oven pan (35 x 27 cm), cut it into squares and serve slightly warm with cream or custard and extra pecan nuts sprinkled on top.

advance preparation: The cake keeps well for up to three days and can also be frozen without the frosting.

280 g (500 ml) cake flour
10 ml bicarbonate of soda
2.5 ml salt
5 ml ground cinnamon
10 ml ground ginger
300 g (375 ml) sugar
3 eggs
250 ml sunflower oil
10 ml vanilla essence
75 g (150 ml) pecan nuts, roughly chopped
75 g (235 ml) desiccated coconut
600 g (700 ml) coarsely grated peeled pears, tightly packed (about 6 or 7 pears)

For the frosting:
450 g (450 ml) smooth cream cheese, drained overnight in a nylon sieve or a piece of muslin
75 g (75 ml) butter, softened
150 g (275 ml) icing sugar
±2.5 ml ground cinnamon
dried pear slices, to decorate (optional)

You will also need:
2 x 23 cm cake tins, at least 6 cm deep, lined with non-stick baking paper

Serves 10

This is a lovely, moist cake that looks spectacular with the dried pear slices. The cream cheese has to be drained overnight, so plan ahead. Do not be tempted to skip this step; it makes a huge difference to the consistency of the frosting.

Grape and Almond Tartlets

For the almond pastry cases, place the flour, sugar and salt in a food processor and pulse to combine. Add the butter and almonds, and process until the mixture resembles fine breadcrumbs. With the motor running, start adding the egg mixture and process just until the dough starts coming together (you may not need all of the liquid). Briefly knead the dough, just to bring it together, then form into a log, about 6 cm in diameter, place in a plastic bag and refrigerate for 1 hour.

Place the pastry log on a lightly floured work surface and cut into 12 rounds. Roll out each round until about 4 mm thick and large enough to fit the tin. Line the tins with pastry and cut off the excess. Refrigerate for at least 30 minutes, or freeze for 15 minutes.

Prick the pastry cases lightly with a fork and line with foil or non-stick baking paper. Fill with dried beans and bake at 190 °C for 12 minutes. Remove the beans and paper and bake for about 6 minutes more until the crust is baked through and begins to brown.

Pastry cream:

Place the egg yolks and castor sugar in a bowl with 30 ml milk and whisk until well combined. Whisk in the cake flour and cornflour. Place the rest of the milk in a small saucepan and bring to the boil. Pour the milk into the egg mixture and mix well. Transfer the mixture to a clean saucepan and bring to the boil over medium heat, stirring continuously. Lower the heat and cook for about 2 minutes until very thick. Remove from the heat and stir in the vanilla and almond essence.

Assembling the tartlets:

Make a glaze by melting the jam with the water and pouring it through a sieve. Leave to cool. Spread the pastry cream into the baked tartlet cases. Arrange the grapes on the pastry cream and brush with the glaze. Sprinkle over the almonds.

For the almond pastry cases:

200 g (365 ml) cake flour
50 g (60 ml) castor sugar
large pinch of salt
120 g butter (125 ml), cut into 1.5 cm cubes and chilled
75 g ground almonds
1 egg, lightly beaten with 30 ml water

For the pastry cream:

3 egg yolks
50 g (60 ml) castor sugar
350 ml milk
35 ml cake flour
30 ml cornflour
5 ml vanilla essence
2.5 ml almond essence

To assemble the tartlets:

30 ml fine grape or other red jam
5 ml water
±200 g seedless grapes (a mixture of green and red looks nice, but use only one colour if you prefer)
±25 g flaked almonds, toasted and roughly crushed

You will also need:

12 metal tart tins, 7.5 cm in diameter and 2 cm deep, preferably loose-bottomed

Makes 12 x 7.5 cm tartlets

cook's note: The ground almonds make this pastry quite soft, so it is important to chill it well before rolling. Do not be alarmed if the pastry cream becomes lumpy while reaching boiling point; simply continue stirring and it will become smooth again. If there are still a few lumps, press the mixture through a sieve or liquidise it. Before using the pastry cream, quickly whiz it in a food processor to make it really smooth.

advance preparation: The pastry will keep in the fridge for at least two days. The raw pastry cases can be frozen for a week or two and the baked cases kept in an airtight container for up to three days. The pastry cream can be made up to two days in advance. Cover and refrigerate, or freeze.

This is a master recipe, which can be altered according to the fruit in season and what you prefer. Other good choices would be gooseberries, raspberries, strawberries, blueberries and kiwi fruit. If you prefer, replace the almond pastry with ordinary shortcrust pastry, and instead of making small tartlets, make one large tart.

Spicy Pear and Macadamia Nut Crumble
with Whisky-Custard Sauce

For the topping, place the flour, oats, sugar, cinnamon, ginger and salt into a food processor and process until well blended. Add the butter and pulse briefly, then add the nuts and pulse once or twice, just to mix them in.

Pears:
Place the pears in a large mixing bowl. Add the lemon juice and rind, sugar, cinnamon and flour, and toss until well mixed. Spoon the pear filling into the prepared dish and sprinkle over the topping. Press the topping down with the palms of your hands. Bake at 190 °C for about 45 minutes until the pears are tender and the topping is golden brown and crisp. Serve warm or at room temperature with the custard sauce or cream.

Whisky-custard sauce:
Whisk everything together.

cook's note: If making the topping by hand, rub the butter into the flour until it resembles fine breadcrumbs, then stir in the oats, sugar, cinnamon, ginger and salt. Chop the nuts a little finer and stir into the crumble mix.

advance preparation: The sauce can be made a day in advance. The crumble topping can be made a couple of hours in advance, but bake the pudding immediately once the topping has been added.

For the topping:
100 g (175 ml) cake flour
45 g (100 ml) oats
100 g (125 ml) brown sugar
7.5 ml ground cinnamon
5 ml ground ginger
1 ml salt
150 g butter, cut into 1.5 cm cubes and chilled
50 g macadamia nuts, roughly chopped

For the pears:
6 ripe but firm pears, peeled, cored and cut into 2.5 cm pieces
15 ml lemon juice
finely grated rind of 1 lemon
30 g (50 ml) brown sugar
2.5 ml ground cinnamon
15 ml cake flour

For the whisky-custard sauce:
500 ml ready-made custard
80 ml cream
60 ml whisky

You will also need:
an ovenproof dish, roughly 20 x 20 cm, greased with butter

Serves 6

Although old-fashioned, a crumble is still a delicious dessert and quick and easy to make. The whisky-laced sauce turns it into something special.

Surprise Granadilla Pudding

175 g (225 ml) castor sugar
3 eggs, separated
175 ml full-cream milk
50 g (90 ml) cake flour
200 ml fresh granadilla juice
finely grated rind of 1 orange
75 g (75 ml) butter, melted
pinch of salt

You will also need:
an 18 cm soufflé or other ovenproof dish with a capacity of 1.25 litres, lightly greased with butter
a roasting tin in which to bake the pudding

Serves 4–6

Place the sugar, egg yolks and 30 ml milk in a large mixing bowl and whisk for about 3 minutes until smooth. Whisk in the flour, the rest of the milk, the granadilla juice, orange rind and melted butter.

Place the egg whites in a large mixing bowl with a pinch of salt. With clean beaters, beat the egg whites until firm, but not quite stiff. Using a large metal spoon, fold the egg whites into the yolk mixture and spoon into the prepared dish. Place the dish in the roasting tin and pour boiling water into the tin to reach halfway up the sides of the dish. Bake at 180 °C for about 45 minutes until the top is a dark golden brown colour and firm to the touch.

cook's note: To remove granadilla pulp from the seeds, pulse very briefly in a food processor, then place in a sieve and press on the solids to extract all the juice. Alternatively, rub through a sieve with a tablespoon of boiling water, which will help to remove the pulp from the seeds.

Granadilla pulp freezes very well. Either scoop it out of the shell, or just freeze the fruit whole.

This is my version of Japie's favourite, a well-known baked pudding that forms its own sauce while baking. Use fresh granadilla juice for a really intense flavour and bright orange colour.

Cauliflower is nothing but cabbage with a college education.

Mark Twain

Winter

fruit

avocados, bananas, gooseberries, grapefruit, guavas, kiwi fruit, kumquats, lemons, naartjies, oranges, papinos, pawpaws, pears

vegetables

beetroot, broccoli, Brussels sprouts, butternut, cabbage (white and red), carrots, cauliflower, green beans, leeks, mushrooms, parsnips, peas, potatoes, pumpkin, spinach, sweet peppers, sweet potatoes, watercress

Moroccan Lamb and Vegetable Soup
with Chickpeas, Lentils and Noodles

Heat half of the olive oil in a large, deep, heavy-bottomed saucepan over medium-high heat. Add the meat and brown well on all sides. Remove the meat from the pan and set aside.

Add more oil to the pan if necessary, then fry the onions, celery and ginger for about 10 minutes until the onions start to soften. Return the meat to the pan, and add the stock and tomatoes. Cover, bring to boiling point and simmer for 45 minutes. Drain the chickpeas, stir into the soup and simmer, covered, for 30 minutes. Add the lentils and simmer for about 20 minutes until the meat, chickpeas and lentils are tender.

Remove the meat from the soup and cut into small pieces. Return the meat to the soup and add the pasta, tomato paste, half of the coriander, and salt and pepper. Stir well, adding more stock or water if the mixture looks too thick. Simmer for about 15 minutes until the pasta is cooked. Add the parsley, lemon rind and juice, and more salt and pepper if necessary. Stir the rest of the coriander into the soup just before serving. Serve with dates and lemon wedges.

cook's note: The chickpeas need to be soaked overnight, so plan accordingly.

It is important that the meat, chickpeas and lentils are tender before adding the pasta, or the pasta will be mushy by the time the other ingredients are cooked.

advance preparation: The soup can be prepared at least two days in advance and can also be frozen.

±45 ml olive oil
250 g stewing lamb, excess fat removed
2 onions, chopped
2 sticks celery, chopped (including leaves)
6 cm piece fresh ginger, peeled and finely chopped
2 litres beef, chicken or vegetable stock
1 x 400 g can chopped tomatoes
175 g chickpeas, soaked overnight in lots of water
125 g lentils
100 g alphabet noodles or other soup pasta
15 ml tomato paste
1 bunch fresh coriander, coarsely chopped (±200 ml)
salt and freshly ground black pepper
handful of fresh Italian parsley, chopped (±100 ml)
finely grated rind of 1 lemon
juice of 1 lemon
fresh dates and lemon wedges, to serve

Serves 6–8

This meal-in-one soup, called harira, is very popular in Morocco, where they even eat it for breakfast. It is traditionally served with fresh dates and lemons, which can be omitted if you prefer, but the soup really benefits from an extra squeeze of lemon at the table. For a vegetarian version, simply leave out the meat. Don't be put off by the long list of ingredients. It is very easy to make and a hit every time I serve it.

Chunky Cauliflower Soup
with Welsh Rarebit Toast

500 ml vegetable stock
1 medium cauliflower, broken into florets
20 g (30 ml) cornflour
500 ml milk
30 g (30 ml) butter
30 ml Maggi™ seasoning
salt and pepper

For the Welsh rarebit toast:
150 g mature Cheddar cheese, finely grated
2 eggs, lightly whisked with a fork
15 ml butter, softened
5 ml mustard powder
salt and freshly ground black pepper
12 slices French loaf, toasted

Serves 4

Heat the stock in a saucepan, add the cauliflower and simmer for about 10 minutes until tender. Mix the cornflour with a little of the milk to form a smooth paste. Add the rest of the milk to the cauliflower and bring to the boil again, then stir in the cornflour paste. Keep stirring until the soup thickens and boils. Turn down the heat and simmer for 5 minutes. Stir in the butter and Maggi™, season the soup with salt and pepper, and serve in warmed soup bowls with the Welsh rarebit toast on the side.

Welsh rarebit toast:
Mix together the cheese, eggs, butter and mustard, and season the mixture lightly with salt and pepper. Place the bread on a baking sheet and spread each slice thickly with the cheese mixture, making sure that all the slices are covered right to the edges or they will burn. Place under a preheated grill for about 3 minutes until the cheese is golden brown.

cook's note: Maggi™ is a liquid seasoning that is available at Chinese shops and most major supermarkets. It is very handy to have in your cupboard for adding flavour to soups, sauces and casseroles.

advance preparation: The soup can be prepared a day in advance and can also be frozen. The toast can be prepared a few hours in advance, ready for grilling.

This soup is amazing; even children who claim not to like cauliflower love it. My mother was taught how to make the soup by the landlady she was living with in Holland shortly after the Second World War. Meat and fresh produce were in short supply. If you were fortunate enough to get hold of a head of cauliflower, you had to stretch it to provide for two suppers. On the one night the landlady would cook the cauliflower as a meal and reserve the water in which it was boiled. On the following night, milk and seasoning would be added to the cauliflower water, which was then thickened with flour and they would enjoy cauliflower soup for supper. The soup remained a favourite dish in our home, but needless to say, with lots of cauliflower in it. Nowadays my mother even adds cream to the soup to enrich it, which you can do too. The Welsh rarebit toast is my own addition.

Broccoli
with Lemon Breadcrumbs

Heat the olive oil in a large frying pan over medium-low heat. Add the breadcrumbs and stir-fry for about 3 minutes until golden brown and crisp. Stir in the lemon rind and set aside.

Steam the broccoli for 5–7 minutes until tender, toss in the melted butter, and season with salt and pepper. Place in a serving dish and sprinkle over the lemon crumbs.

cook's note: When buying broccoli make sure that it shows no signs of yellowing and that the stalks snap easily, an indication that it is fresh.

advance preparation: The breadcrumbs can be prepared a day in advance. Store in an airtight container.

30 ml olive oil
50 g (200 ml) fresh white breadcrumbs (about 2 slices of bread)
finely grated rind of 1 lemon
400 g broccoli, broken into florets
30 g (30 ml) butter, melted
salt and freshly ground black pepper

Serves 4

Broccoli is very good for you, being rich in antioxidants as well as a good source of fibre. Steaming is the best way of cooking in order to preserve its good qualities.

Tuna and Avocado Melts

Brush the bread with olive oil. Toast on both sides under a grill or in a very hot, ridged cast iron grill pan until crisp.

Place the tuna in a mixing bowl, add the mayonnaise and mix well. Add the avocado, parsley, lemon juice, salt and pepper, and combine lightly. Spread the mixture on the toasted bread and place on a baking sheet. Sprinkle the cheese on top and place under a preheated grill for about 3 minutes until golden brown. Sprinkle over some paprika, garnish with parsley and serve immediately.

Serve these as a quick, light supper with a tomato salad, or make them smaller and serve as a pre-dinner snack with a glass of wine.

8 slices ciabatta bread
±30 ml olive oil
1 x 170 g can shredded tuna in water, drained
45 ml mayonnaise
1 avocado, cut into 1 cm pieces
50 ml roughly chopped fresh Italian parsley, plus a few extra leaves for garnishing
lemon juice to taste
salt and freshly ground black pepper
50 g Cheddar cheese, grated
paprika, for sprinkling

Makes 8

Venison Pie

For the pastry, place the flour and salt in a food processor and pulse to blend. Add the butter and process until the mixture resembles fine breadcrumbs.

Lightly beat the egg, vinegar and water together. With the motor running, start adding the egg mixture and process just until the dough comes together (you may not require all of the liquid). Form the dough into a disc, place in a plastic bag and refrigerate for at least 1 hour.

Filling:
Heat 30 ml oil in the casserole over medium heat. Add the bacon, onions, carrots and garlic, and cook for about 10 minutes until the onions start to soften. Add the pork fat and stir-fry for a further 5 minutes. Remove the vegetable mixture from the pot and set aside.

Add more oil to the pot and, working in batches, brown the meat over high heat, adding more oil if necessary. Remove the meat from the pot and set aside.

Deglaze the pot with the wine and add the stock. Return the meat and vegetable mixture to the pot, add the cloves, ginger, mixed herbs, dried oregano, bay leaves, orange rind, salt and some pepper, and bring to the boil. Cover the pot and cook at 150 °C until the meat is very tender, giving it a stir every hour or so. The cooking process may take up to 5 hours, depending on the cut of meat you use.

When the meat is tender, remove the pot from the oven and let it cool down slightly. Coarsely shred the meat, discarding the bones and sinews. Return the meat to the pot, add the Worcestershire sauce and reheat. If the meat is too saucy, let it simmer, uncovered, until reduced to a suitable consistency.

Taste and add more salt and pepper if necessary. Spoon the mixture into the pie dish and let it cool down.

Rich shortcrust pastry:
- 280 g (500 ml) cake flour
- 3 ml salt
- 200 g (210 ml) butter, cut into 1.5 cm cubes and chilled
- 1 egg
- 7.5 ml white wine vinegar
- 50 ml ice-cold water

For the filling:
- ±60 ml olive oil
- 250 g streaky bacon, chopped
- 3 onions, chopped
- 2 large carrots, diced
- 3 large cloves garlic, roughly chopped
- 75 g pork fat, finely diced
- 1.5 kg venison meat, such as springbok, cut into 5 cm pieces
- 250 ml red wine
- 1.25 litres beef stock
- 10 ml whole cloves
- 5 ml ground ginger
- 15 ml chopped fresh mixed herbs, e.g. rosemary and thyme or 5 ml dried mixed herbs
- 5 ml dried oregano
- 3 bay leaves
- 3 strips of orange rind
- 2.5 ml salt
- freshly ground black pepper
- 30 ml Worcestershire sauce

To assemble the pie:
1 egg, lightly whisked

You will also need:
a large, heavy-bottomed casserole pot with a lid for cooking the meat
a 20 cm round pie dish for baking the pie

Serves 8

Assembling the pie:

On a lightly floured surface roll the pastry into a circle about 3 cm larger than the size of the dish. Brush the rim of the dish with the whisked egg, lay the pastry over the dish and cut off the excess. Crimp the edges around the rim to seal.

Brush the pastry with whisked egg and, using a sharp knife, cut small slits in the top of the pie. Roll out the pastry trimmings, cut out shapes and place on top of the pastry. Brush the shapes with egg. Refrigerate the pie for 30 minutes or place in the freezer for 20 minutes. Brush with more whisked egg and bake for about 30 minutes at 200 °C until golden brown.

cook's note: If you find it difficult to roll out the pastry, try rolling it between two sheets of greaseproof paper.

advance preparation: The pastry can be kept in the fridge for a day or two and can also be frozen. The meat can be cooked a day in advance, and can also be frozen. The pie can be assembled, ready for baking, a few hours in advance. Keep it refrigerated.

For as long as I can remember, my mother has been cooking venison this way, and I have always loved it. Making it in pie form is my own version. I used springbok for this pie, but you can use any game meat of your choice.
The pastry is to die for; it almost melts in your mouth. I use it for other pies as well, such as empanadas (see page 112).

Lamb Tagine
with Prunes and Almonds

Heat 30 ml oil in a large, heavy-bottomed saucepan, add the onions and cook for about 10 minutes over low heat until soft. Add the garlic, cumin, paprika, ginger, pepper, saffron or turmeric and cloves, and stir-fry for a further 2 minutes. Increase the heat, add the lamb and cook it for about 5 minutes to absorb the flavour of the spices, stirring constantly and adding more oil if necessary.

Stir in the orange juice, cinnamon stick, salt and water, cover, and simmer until the lamb is tender, 1–1½ hours. Add more water if it looks dry.

Meanwhile, place the prunes in a small bowl, cover with boiling water and let it stand for 30 minutes.

When the meat is tender, drain the prunes and add to the lamb together with the honey, ground cinnamon and almonds. Stir in the chopped coriander and serve.

advance preparation: The tagine can be prepared a day in advance. It can also be frozen before adding the prunes, honey, almonds and coriander. Defrost overnight, place in an ovenproof dish, add the prunes, honey and almonds and reheat at 140 °C until piping hot. Stir in the coriander before serving.

±45 ml olive oil
2 onions, finely chopped
2 cloves garlic, crushed
10 ml ground cumin
5 ml paprika
5 ml ground ginger
1.25 ml coarsely ground black pepper
2.5 ml ground saffron or turmeric
pinch of ground cloves
750 g deboned shoulder of lamb, trimmed of excess fat and cut into 3 cm pieces
125 ml orange juice
1 cinnamon stick
1.25 ml salt
125 ml water
100 g prunes
15 ml honey
1.25 ml ground cinnamon
50 g whole blanched almonds, roasted
60 ml roughly chopped fresh coriander

Serves 4

Tagine is the name of a Moroccan conical earthenware dish, as well as the stew that is cooked in it. The sweetness in this stew is typical of many Moroccan dishes. Saffron, the orangy-red stamens of a purple crocus flower, is the most expensive spice in the world. It is intensely fragrant, with a slightly bitter taste, and is widely used in Middle Eastern dishes, as well as in French seafood stews and Spanish paella. It can be replaced with turmeric, as indicated in the recipe. This dish is a good choice when entertaining, as it tastes even better if cooked a day in advance. Serve with couscous with spring onions.

Thai Vegetable Curry
with Peanuts and Lemony Jasmine Rice

Heat the oil in a large frying pan or wok over fairly high heat, add the peppers and stir-fry for about 5 minutes until they start to soften. Add the garlic and fry for another minute or two, then add the curry paste and about 30 ml coconut milk. Stir until the curry paste has dissolved. Add the rest of the coconut milk, the stock, fish sauce and brown sugar, and give it a stir. Add the butternut, cover the pan and simmer for 12 minutes. Add the green beans and simmer, uncovered, for about another 10 minutes until all the vegetables are tender. Taste and add salt and pepper if necessary and lemon juice to taste.

Reserve a few coriander leaves for garnishing, then roughly chop the rest and stir into the curry. Spoon into a serving dish and sprinkle the peanuts and reserved coriander leaves on top. Serve with the lemony jasmine rice.

Lemony jasmine rice:
Place the rice, water and salt in a large saucepan. Bring to the boil, cover and simmer over low heat for about 15 minutes until the rice is tender and the water absorbed. Remove from the heat, transfer to a large bowl and leave to cool.

Heat the oil in a large frying pan over medium-high heat. Add the cooled rice to the pan, breaking it up with your fingers to separate the grains. Sprinkle over the lemon juice and stir-fry the rice for about 5 minutes until heated through. Remove from the heat, stir in the lemon rind and serve immediately, garnished with the lemon wedges.

cook's note: Jasmine rice is moist in texture and tends to cling together when cooked; it will not be fluffy. Jasmine rice is available at most supermarkets.

advance preparation: The rice can be cooked a day in advance. Cover and refrigerate.

30 ml peanut oil
2 red peppers, cut into strips
3 cloves garlic, crushed
10 ml red curry paste
600 ml coconut milk
100 ml vegetable or chicken stock
25 ml fish sauce
30 ml brown sugar
1 kg butternut, peeled and cut into 2 cm pieces
300 g green beans, trimmed and cut into 3 cm pieces
salt and freshly ground black pepper
±20 ml lemon juice
handful of coriander leaves
70 g (100 ml) roasted peanuts, roughly chopped

For the lemony jasmine rice:
250 g (280 ml) jasmine rice
450 ml water
4 ml salt
30 ml peanut or olive oil
±20 ml lemon juice (adjust according to taste)
finely grated rind of 1 large lemon
a lemon wedge or two, to garnish

Serves 4–6

Fish sauce, made from pulverised, salted, fermented fish, is widely used in Thai and Vietnamese cuisine, adding a rich, salty flavour to soups, sauces and dressings. Use soy sauce as a substitute, but it will taste a little different. Fish sauce is available at most major and Chinese supermarkets. If someone is allergic to peanuts, replace the peanut oil with grapeseed or olive oil, and the peanuts with roasted pepitas (pumpkin seeds).

Picadillo Shepherd's Pie
with Parsley Potato Topping

750 g potatoes
60 g (60 ml) butter
±75 ml milk
salt and freshly ground black pepper
50 ml chopped fresh Italian parsley
1 quantity picadillo (see page 122)

You will also need:
an ovenproof dish, roughly 20 x 20 cm, lightly greased

Serves 4–6

Boil the potatoes in their skins until tender, then drain, peel and mash. Place the mashed potato in a saucepan over low heat and stir in the butter. Add just enough of the milk to make it soft and spreadable. Season with salt and pepper, and stir in the parsley.

Place the picadillo in the prepared dish and spread the mashed potato over it. Make a crisscross pattern on top with a fork and bake for about 30 minutes at 200 °C until golden brown and crisp.

This pie is ideal for informal entertaining as it can be prepared in the morning and baked just before you want to eat. Serve with broccoli with lemon breadcrumbs (see page 56).

Roasted Butternut Salad
with Pecan Nuts and Feta

±600 g butternut, peeled and cut into 1 cm thick slices
15 ml olive oil
5 ml ground cumin
salt and freshly ground black pepper
large handful of rocket leaves
75 g feta cheese, crumbled
40 g pecan nuts, toasted and roughly chopped
finely grated rind of 1 small lemon

You will also need:
a large, shallow roasting tin, lightly greased or sprayed with non-stick cooking spray

Serves 4–6

Place the butternut in a large mixing bowl, add the oil, cumin and salt and pepper, and toss to coat. Spread the butternut out in the roasting tin and roast at 200 °C for about 30 minutes until cooked and crisp. Leave to cool slightly.

Place the rocket leaves on a large serving platter and arrange the butternut on top. Scatter over the feta and pecan nuts, and sprinkle the lemon rind on top. Serve warm or at room temperature.

advance preparation: The butternut can be roasted a few hours in advance.

The combination of ingredients in this salad is just terrific. The butternut can be replaced with orange-flesh sweet potatoes if preferred.

Chicken Pie

with Roasted Peppers and Feta

Place each chicken breast between two sheets of clingfilm and bash with a rolling pin to flatten, about 1 cm thick. Season with salt and pepper and sprinkle with thyme.

Heat 15 ml olive oil in a large frying pan over medium-high heat. Fry the chicken in batches until browned on both sides and barely cooked, about 3 minutes on each side, adding more oil if necessary. Remove from the pan, leave to cool and cut each breast diagonally in three.

Dry the roasted peppers with kitchen paper, cut into 3 cm wide strips and season lightly with salt and pepper.

Open the pastry on a lightly floured work surface and roll into a rectangular shape, roughly 35 x 25 cm (it will probably be almost that size, so you won't have to do much rolling). Transfer to the prepared baking sheet. Spread the pesto down the long centre third of the pastry. Arrange half of the chicken on the pesto, leaving a small border at each short end. Cover with half the peppers and half the feta. Repeat with the rest of the chicken, peppers and feta. Brush the edges of the pastry with the beaten egg.

Fold the two long edges of the pastry over the filling. Don't worry if they don't quite meet; it is fine if there is a small gap in the middle with a bit of filling showing. Crimp the edges of the pastry with your fingers. Seal the short ends and cut off the excess pastry. Brush the pastry with the beaten egg and sprinkle over the poppy seeds. Bake at 200 °C for 30–35 minutes until the pastry is cooked through, golden brown and crisp.

Leave to stand for 5 minutes, cut into thick slices and place on a serving plate. Serve with roasted tomato and pepper sauce (see page 66).

advance preparation: The peppers can be roasted and the chicken cooked a day in advance. The pie can be completed, ready for baking, a few hours in advance. Keep refrigerated. It can also be frozen.

450 g chicken breasts, skinless and deboned
salt and freshly ground black pepper
5 ml fresh thyme leaves
±30 ml olive oil
2 large red peppers, roasted and peeled (see page 9)
400 g ready-made puff pastry, defrosted if frozen
30 ml sun-dried tomato pesto (see page 102), or store-bought pesto
125 g feta cheese, dried with kitchen paper, thinly sliced or crumbled
1 egg, lightly beaten with a fork
poppy seeds, to sprinkle on top

You will also need:
a large baking sheet, lightly greased or sprayed with non-stick cooking spray

Serves 4

This utterly delicious pie is great for entertaining as it can be completed a few hours in advance and kept in the fridge, ready for baking.

Italian Meatballs

with Roasted Tomato and Pepper Sauce

Heat 30 ml olive oil in a saucepan and cook the onion for about 10 minutes until soft but not brown. Add the garlic and cook for another minute, then remove from the heat and set aside to cool.

Place the breadcrumbs in a bowl, stir in the milk and leave to soak for 10 minutes.

Place the mince in a mixing bowl and add the soaked breadcrumbs, the cooled onion and garlic, Parmesan cheese, egg, parsley, lemon rind, nutmeg, salt and pepper. Lightly mix with your hands until well combined (do not over mix).

Wet your hands to prevent the mixture from sticking, and form small balls, about the size of golf balls. Flatten them slightly with your fingers and place on a large tray. Heat about 45 ml olive oil in a large saucepan over medium heat and fry the meatballs in batches for 5–10 minutes until golden brown on both sides, adding more oil if necessary.

To serve, add the meatballs to the sauce, cover and simmer gently for about 15 minutes until the meatballs are heated through. Garnish with chopped parsley leaves and serve on soft polenta or pasta. Sprinkle with the extra Parmesan.

Roasted tomato and pepper sauce:

Arrange the tomatoes cut side up in the roasting tin, drizzle with about 15 ml oil, sprinkle with sugar and season lightly with salt and pepper. Roast at 200 °C for about 30 minutes until the tomatoes start to char at the edges.

Meanwhile, heat 30 ml olive oil in a large saucepan and cook the onion for about 10 minutes until tender. Add the garlic and cook for another minute.

Transfer the onion and garlic to a food processor. Add the roasted tomatoes, canned tomatoes and roasted pepper, and process until quite smooth but still with some texture. Return the mixture to the saucepan, add the stock and heat gently. Stir in the parsley, taste, and adjust the seasoning if necessary. Add a little more stock if the sauce is too thick.

±90 ml olive oil
1 large onion, finely chopped
2 cloves garlic, crushed
40 g (150 ml) fresh white breadcrumbs
60 ml milk
500 g lean minced beef
60 g (75 ml) freshly grated Parmesan cheese, plus extra for sprinkling
1 egg, lightly whisked
100 ml chopped fresh Italian parsley, plus a few extra leaves for garnishing
finely grated rind of 1 large lemon
pinch of nutmeg
4 ml salt
freshly ground black pepper

For the roasted tomato and pepper sauce (makes about 1 litre):

500 g plum tomatoes, halved
±45 ml olive oil
pinch of brown sugar
salt and freshly ground black pepper
1 onion, finely chopped
2 cloves garlic, crushed
1 x 400 g can chopped tomatoes
1 large red pepper, roasted, peeled and sliced (see page 9)
±100 ml vegetable stock
50 ml chopped fresh Italian parsley

You will also need:

a greased, shallow roasting tin

Serves 4–6

The fried onion, lemon rind and Parmesan cheese in this recipe make the meatballs particularly flavourful. Serve with soft polenta with leeks (see page 68) and you have comfort food at its best.

cook's note: It is important not to overcrowd the pan when frying the meatballs or they will steam and not brown. Instead of frying them, the meatballs can also be baked on an oiled baking sheet at 180 °C for about 25 minutes.

advance preparation: The meatballs can be shaped and kept overnight in the fridge (in their raw state). They can also be frozen; defrost before cooking. The meatballs and sauce can be cooked a day in advance. Gently reheat the meatballs in the sauce before serving.

Soft Polenta
with Leeks

Heat the oil in a large saucepan over medium-low heat. Add the leeks and cook for about 10 minutes until soft but not brown. Remove the leeks from the pan and set aside.

Pour the stock and milk into the pan and bring to the boil. Add the polenta in a steady stream, whisking or stirring constantly with a wooden spoon. When all the polenta has been added, cover the saucepan and turn down the heat. Cook for about 20 minutes until the mixture is thick and creamy, stirring often and adding more stock or water if it looks too thick. The polenta should have the consistency of soft porridge.

Remove the pan from the heat and stir in the butter, Parmesan (if using) and cooked leeks. Season to taste with salt and pepper.

cook's note: Take care when cooking the leeks not to let them brown. If they do start browning, add a few drops of water and turn down the heat. It is better to remove the leeks from the pan when they are cooked and adding them again later; this way they add a bit of texture to the polenta.

advance preparation: The leeks can be cooked a day in advance. Cover and refrigerate.

45 ml olive oil
200 g (about 3) leeks, sliced
900 ml vegetable stock
450 ml milk
165 g (225 ml) polenta
30 g (30 ml) butter
60 g (75 ml) freshly grated Parmesan cheese (optional)
salt and freshly ground black pepper

Serves 4–6

Polenta is a porridge made from yellow or white maize meal (yes, it is basically 'mieliepap'!). It has been a staple food in northern Italy for ages, and is traditionally eaten in winter as wonderful comfort food. It tastes rather bland on its own, but the addition of butter, cheese, herbs and other ingredients makes it really tasty.

In this recipe the polenta is made into a soft porridge, which is great when eaten with saucy meat or chicken dishes. Polenta can also be left to cool and set, and then grilled or fried (see page 40). In some parts of northern Italy slices of cold polenta are eaten as an alternative to bread.

White Chocolate Meringues
with Kiwi Fruit

3 egg whites
pinch of salt
165 g (200 ml) castor sugar
few drops of green food colouring
80 g white chocolate
150 ml mascarpone
100 ml ready-made custard
4 kiwi fruit, peeled and sliced

You will also need:
2 baking sheets lined with
non-stick baking paper

Serves 8

Place the egg whites in a large bowl with a pinch of salt and whisk until stiff. Add 30 ml castor sugar, whisk again until stiff, then add the rest of the sugar bit by bit, whisking well after each addition. The mixture must be very stiff and glossy. Whisk in the food colouring.

Spoon the meringue into eight equal-sized rounds on the paper-lined baking sheets. With the back of a spoon, make an indentation in each round. Bake at 110 °C for about 2 hours until crisp. Turn off the oven and leave the meringues to cool in the oven for 1 hour. Transfer to racks to cool down completely.

Melt the chocolate and paint the indentations in the meringues with the chocolate. Leave to stand at room temperature until the chocolate has set, which may take up to an hour, depending on the ambient temperature.

Whisk together the mascarpone and custard, and fill each meringue with some of the mixture. Place a few slices of kiwi fruit on top.

cook's note: White chocolate seizes more easily than dark chocolate, so make sure you do not overheat it when melting.

Store leftover egg whites in the fridge for making meringues, or freeze them. One egg white equals 30 ml or 30 g.

advance preparation: The unfilled meringues can be stored in an airtight container for up to a week. Once painted with the chocolate, use within a day.

Meringue is always popular for dessert. Here I have combined it with kiwi fruit, the acidity of which goes exceptionally well with the sweetness of the meringue.

I like to add a few drops of green food colouring to the meringue mixture so that they come out a pale green colour, which looks pretty with the pale filling and bright green kiwi fruit.

Rustic Pear and Chocolate Tart

Place the flour, sugar and salt in a food processor. Add the butter and process until the mixture resembles fine breadcrumbs. Add the egg and process just until the dough comes together. Form into a disc, place in a plastic bag and refrigerate for 1 hour.

On a lightly floured work surface roll out the dough in a circular shape until about 4 mm thick and 28 cm in diameter. Place the dough on the prepared baking sheet.

Filling:
Mix the lemon juice and 5 ml of the brown sugar in a large mixing bowl. Peel and quarter the pears, remove the cores and cut the fruit into 2.5 cm pieces. Add to the lemon juice mixture together with the flour and toss to coat. Stir in the chocolate.

Pile the filling onto the rolled pastry, leaving a clear border of 5 cm all around. Fold the pastry border up over the fruit, pressing it down lightly and leaving the centre open. Dot the fruit with the butter.

Make a glaze by whisking the egg yolk with 5 ml water. Brush the pastry with the egg glaze and sprinkle the remaining 45 ml brown sugar over the whole tart, pastry and fruit. Bake at 200 °C for about 40 minutes until golden brown and bubbling.

Dust with icing sugar and serve lukewarm with crème fraîche.

cook's note: It is important to chill the pastry really well before rolling it out, or it will be too soft to handle. Use a light rolling action, no pressure, and keep the pastry on the move while rolling, in other words, give it a quarter turn every now and then to prevent it from sticking. If you still find this difficult, you may consider rolling out the pastry between two sheets of greaseproof paper.

advance preparation: The pastry can be kept in the fridge for a couple of days and can also be frozen.

For the pastry:
170 g (310 ml) cake flour
50 g (60 ml) castor sugar
pinch of salt
120 g (125 ml) butter, cut into 1.5 cm cubes and chilled
1 egg

For the filling:
10 ml lemon juice
45 g (50 ml) brown sugar
4 large ripe but firm pears
15 ml cake flour
75 g dark chocolate, roughly chopped
50 g (50 ml) butter, cut into small pieces
1 egg yolk
icing sugar, for dusting
crème fraîche, to serve

You will also need:
a rimmed baking sheet lightly greased with butter

Serves 8

The tart can be served with afternoon coffee or as a dessert. My husband, who does not have a sweet tooth, loves it for dessert, and so will anybody who is not fond of overly sweet desserts. As the name says, this is a rustic tart, so do not be concerned if it cracks a bit while baking. The tart tastes best slightly warm, about 10 minutes after being removed from the oven.

Individual Malva Puddings
with Candied Citrus Rind

Sift the flour, bicarbonate of soda and salt together. Place the milk in a jug and stir in the vinegar.

In a large mixing bowl, whisk the castor sugar and eggs until pale and fluffy. Add the jam, butter and lemon rind, and whisk again until well mixed. Using a large metal spoon, fold the flour mixture into the egg mixture alternately with the milk mixture, in two additions each. Pour into the greased moulds, dividing it equally. Bake at 180 °C for 20–25 minutes until a skewer inserted in the centre comes out clean.

Sauce:
Prepare the sauce while the puddings are baking. Place all the ingredients in a saucepan. Stir over low heat until the butter and sugar melt; don't let it boil. Keep the sauce warm.

As soon as the puddings come out of the oven, prick each one a few times with a skewer. Gradually pour over the warm sauce, leaving it to be absorbed before continuing. Leave the puddings to stand for 10 minutes before turning out.

To turn out, invert the mould into the palm of your hand, give it a shake and it should slide out easily. Place on serving plates, decorate with the candied citrus rind and serve with custard or ice cream.

Candied citrus rind:
Use a potato peeler to cut strips of rind from the orange and lemon, working from the top to the bottom of the fruit. Be careful not to cut into the white pith. If there are any white bits, scrape them off with a serrated knife otherwise the rind may taste bitter. Cut the rind into fine strips (it doesn't matter if they look irregular).

Place the sugar and the water in a small saucepan. Stir over low heat until the sugar has dissolved. Add the strips of rind and simmer until tender, about 5 minutes. Remove from the pan and drain in a sieve.

200 g (365 ml) cake flour
5 ml bicarbonate of soda
2.5 ml salt
200 ml milk
5 ml white vinegar
210 g (250 ml) castor sugar
2 eggs
15 ml smooth apricot jam
30 g (30 ml) butter, softened
grated rind of 1 large lemon

For the sauce:
250 ml cream
110 g (115 ml) butter
60 g (75 ml) sugar
125 ml water
10 ml vanilla essence

For the candied citrus rind decoration (optional):
1 orange
1 lemon
80 g (100 ml) sugar
100 ml water
±25 g (±30 ml) castor sugar

You will also need:
8 dariole or other ovenproof moulds with a capacity of 200 ml, sprayed with non-stick cooking spray

Makes 8 individual puddings

This is a traditional South African pudding, also known as church pudding because of its popularity at church bazaars. It is, in fact, simply a baked sponge pudding soaked with a rich sweet sauce. You can make one large pudding if you prefer, but the individual ones look especially attractive when plated and topped with candied rind. Making the candied rind is a bit of extra work and not essential, but it is well worth the effort in order to add a splash of colour to an otherwise quite dull looking dessert.

Place the castor sugar in a small bowl. Add half of the drained rind and toss to coat with sugar. Place on greaseproof paper. Repeat with the other strips of rind and leave for about 2 hours on the paper to dry out slightly. Store in an airtight container.

cook's note: Dariole moulds are small, steep-sided cylindrical moulds made of metal, used for making puddings, cakes or pastries.

advance preparation: The puddings can be prepared a day in advance. Reheat at 180 °C for about 10 minutes. They can also be frozen. The candied rind can be kept in an airtight container for a week or two.

Spring in the world!
And all things are made new!

Richard Hovey

Spring

fruit

bananas, blueberries, cherries, kumquats, mulberries, pineapples, raspberries, rhubarb, strawberries

vegetables

asparagus, baby marrows, beetroot, cauliflower, cucumber, green beans, mangetout, mushrooms, peas, spinach, sugar snap peas, tomatoes

Bacon and Asparagus Muffins

Cut the asparagus into 2.5 cm pieces (if using thick ones, halve them first lengthways, then cut into pieces).

Heat 15 ml oil in a large frying pan over medium heat, add the asparagus and a little salt and pepper, and stir-fry for about 5 minutes until tender-crisp. Remove the asparagus from the pan and set aside. Add more oil if necessary and fry the bacon in the same pan for about 5 minutes until slightly crisp but not hard. Chop the bacon and set aside with the asparagus.

Sift the flour and salt together in a large bowl. Whisk the buttermilk, eggs and mustard together just until well mixed. Lightly stir the buttermilk mixture into the dry ingredients with a large metal spoon, then stir in the butter. Add the bacon and asparagus and mix in lightly.

Spoon into the prepared muffin tray, filling each cup about two-thirds. Bake at 200 °C for about 20 minutes until a tester inserted into the centre of the muffins comes out clean. Cool on a wire rack.

cook's note: The muffin mixture should be mixed lightly; too much mixing will make the muffins heavy.

advance preparation: Muffins are best eaten fresh from the oven, but they can be frozen for about a month. Reheat at 180 °C for about 10 minutes.

200 g fresh green asparagus, trimmed
±30 ml olive oil
salt and freshly ground black pepper
125 g rindless smoked bacon
350 g (640 ml) self-raising flour
1.25 ml salt
250 ml buttermilk (not low fat)
2 eggs
30 ml grainy mustard
125 g (130 ml) butter, melted

You will also need:
a 12-cup muffin tray, each cup with a capacity of 80 ml, sprayed with non-stick cooking spray

Makes 12

These muffins are great for breakfast or brunch. Serve them fresh from the oven with grated mature Cheddar cheese.

Caramelised Onion, Asparagus and Gruyère Tartlets

Place the flour and salt in a food processor and pulse to blend. Add the butter and process until the mixture resembles fine breadcrumbs. With the motor running, start adding the whisked egg and process just until the dough comes together (you may not require all of the egg mixture). Form the pastry into a log, about 7 cm in diameter, place in a plastic bag and refrigerate for 30 minutes.

Cut the pastry log into eight rounds. On a lightly floured surface, roll out each round until about 4 mm thick and large enough to fit the tartlet tins. Line the tins with pastry, trim the excess and refrigerate for at least 30 minutes, or freeze for 15 minutes.

Prick the pastry cases with a fork and line with foil or non-stick baking paper. Fill with dried beans and bake at 190 °C for 12 minutes. Remove the beans and bake for about 6 minutes longer until light biscuit brown.

Filling:
Steam the asparagus until just tender, 1–2 minutes. Refresh under cold, running water, drain and dry on kitchen paper. If necessary, cut to a size that will fit into the tins.

Heat the oil and butter in a large frying pan over medium heat, add the onions and cook for about 5 minutes while stirring. Reduce the heat to low, cover the pan and cook the onions for about 30 minutes until soft and translucent, stirring occasionally. Stir in the sugar, increase the heat to medium and cook the onions for about another 45 minutes until golden brown and caramelised. Remove from the heat, stir in the thyme and season with salt and pepper. Roughly chop the onions (to make them easier to eat) and set aside to cool.

For the pastry:
280 g (500 ml) cake flour
2.5 ml salt
150 g cold butter, cut into 1.5 cm cubes
2 eggs, lightly whisked with 5 ml water

For the filling:
24 (about 120 g) fresh green asparagus tips
30 ml olive oil
30 g (30 ml) butter
750 g onions, peeled, halved and thinly sliced crosswise
15 ml brown sugar
15 ml fresh thyme leaves
salt and freshly ground black pepper
80 g gruyère cheese, finely grated
150 ml sour cream
150 ml full-cream milk
2 whole eggs and 2 egg yolks

You will also need:
8 x 10 cm metal tart tins, preferably loose-bottomed ones

Makes 8 tartlets

These delightful tartlets can be served as a starter, a light lunch, or a main course for vegetarians. You can replace the gruyère cheese with mature Cheddar.
The tartlets are very easy to prepare, the only task that takes a while is slicing the onions. A mandolin (see page 9) will do the job in next to no time. It is a good idea to get the onions started first, as they cook for quite a long time. But since they don't need constant attention, prepare the rest of the filling while they are cooking.
If possible, use lemon thyme for this recipe; it combines really well with the onions and asparagus.

Spread the onions in the baked tartlet cases and sprinkle over the cheese, dividing it equally. Whisk together the sour cream, milk, eggs and egg yolks until smooth and season the mixture with salt and pepper. Pour the egg mixture into the tartlet cases, filling them almost to the top. Arrange three asparagus tips on each one and bake at 180 °C for about 20 minutes until the tarts are puffed and golden brown.

cook's note: Do not be alarmed if it looks like a lot of onions; they shrink remarkably while cooking.

Try to buy asparagus tips that are quite thin, otherwise you will have difficulty fitting them into the tins. If you buy whole asparagus, use the tips for this recipe and reserve the rest for another dish, for instance a stir-fry or an omelette.

advance preparation: The pastry keeps well in the fridge for a day or two and can also be frozen. The onions can be cooked and the tartlet cases baked a day or two in advance. Refrigerate the onions and keep the tartlet cases in an airtight container. The asparagus can be steamed a few hours in advance.

Dragon Wings with Tzatziki

Place the tomato sauce, oil, sugar and curry paste in a saucepan over low heat and stir for about 5 minutes until the sugar and curry paste have dissolved. Remove from the heat and stir in the lemon rind. Leave to cool.

Place the chicken wings in a mixing bowl, add the cooled curry paste mixture and toss to coat. Cover and marinate for at least 2 hours or overnight. Add the lemon wedges and bay leaves to the marinated chicken and toss in the marinade.

To braai/barbecue the chicken, thread a chicken wing, bay leaf and lemon wedge on each skewer. Season the chicken with salt and cook over hot coals, turning occasionally, for about 30 minutes until well browned and cooked through.

To cook in the oven, cover a rimmed baking tray with foil and grease lightly (the foil is to prevent you spending the rest of the day scrubbing the tray!). Spread the wings out in a single layer on the tray and season with salt. Tuck the lemon wedges and bay leaves in between and bake at 190 °C for 35–40 minutes until cooked and slightly charred. Serve with the tzatziki.

Tzatziki:
Mix together the yoghurt, cucumber, oil, garlic and mint or dill. Add salt and pepper to taste.

cook's note: Curry pastes differ in strength, so you may have to adjust the amount in the recipe, according to the brand you use and your personal preference. The amount specified normally makes a rather mild curry dish. Curry paste is available from Chinese supermarkets and from most major supermarkets.

Use full-cream yoghurt for the tzatziki for a rich, creamy taste. Don't skip draining the yoghurt even if it does not look watery – it does make a huge difference. It's also important to get rid of the cucumber seeds or the tzatziki will have a watery texture.

advance preparation: The chicken can be cooked a day in advance. Leave to cool, then cover and refrigerate. Reheat at 190 °C until piping hot. The tzatziki can be prepared at least a day in advance (in fact, it is better to prepare it a day in advance to let the flavours develop). Cover and refrigerate.

75 ml tomato sauce
50 ml olive oil
45 g (50 ml) brown sugar
10 ml red curry paste
finely grated rind of 1 lemon
16 chicken wings, tips removed if desired
2 small lemons, each cut into 8 wedges
16 bay leaves
salt

For the tzatziki:
300 ml Greek yoghurt, drained overnight in a nylon sieve or muslin cloth
1 English cucumber, peeled, seeded and finely diced
15 ml olive oil
1 or 2 cloves garlic, crushed
50 ml finely chopped fresh mint or dill
sea salt and freshly ground black pepper

Serves 8

Tzatziki is a simple Middle Eastern dish of cucumber and yoghurt, often seen on menus in Greek restaurants. It goes very well with hot and spicy foods, as with these chicken wings.

If you want to braai/barbecue the wings you will need sixteen long metal or strong wooden skewers. Provide lots of napkins and lemon finger bowls for cleaning sticky fingers.

Steak Sandwiches

with Grilled Onion and Garlic and Herb Butter

In a small bowl, mix together the butter, garlic, thyme, oregano, lemon rind and lots of black pepper. Cover and refrigerate until needed.

To keep the onion slices intact, press two toothpicks horizontally and from opposite sides into each slice. Place the onions in a mixing bowl, add the olive oil and salt and pepper, and toss to coat. Cook on the braai/barbecue for about 25 minutes until softened, turning occasionally. (If cooking indoors, roast at 200 °C for about 45 minutes.) Peel off the outer layer, separate the onion into rings and set aside.

Braai/barbecue the steak until done to your preference, about 3 minutes on each side for medium-rare. Spread the steak generously with the garlic and herb butter and let it rest for a few minutes.

Meanwhile, halve the loaves horizontally, then cut each one in half again crosswise. Toast the bread and spread with garlic and herb butter while still hot. Slice the steak thinly against the grain. Pile the tomato, steak and onion on the toasted bread and serve immediately.

advance preparation: The garlic and herb butter can be refrigerated for a day or two and can also be frozen. Form into a log, cover with plastic wrap and refrigerate or freeze.

100 g (100 ml) butter, softened
2 cloves garlic, crushed
10 ml chopped fresh thyme
5 ml dried oregano
finely grated rind of 1 lemon
freshly ground black pepper
4 onions, unpeeled, cut into 1.5 cm thick slices, ends discarded
30 ml olive oil
salt
700 g porterhouse or rump steak, trimmed of excess fat
2 small French loaves
3 or 4 tomatoes, sliced

Makes 8 sandwiches

A little meat goes a long way in this delicious sandwich. The steak tastes best when done on the braai/barbecue, but you can of course also char grill or pan-fry it. Buy a thick piece of steak for a juicy end result.

Spring Onion Mashed Potato

750 g potatoes
40 g (40 ml) butter
190 ml milk or cream
1 bunch spring onions, thinly sliced (include some of the green parts)
salt and freshly ground black pepper

Serves 4–6

Boil the potatoes in their skins until tender, then drain, peel and mash them.

Place the butter and the milk or cream in a small saucepan over low heat. As soon as the butter has melted, stir in the spring onions and add the mixture to the mashed potato. Mix well, season with salt and pepper and reheat gently.

advance preparation: The mashed potato can be prepared a couple of hours in advance. Reheat over low heat while stirring constantly.

This is such a simple dish, but so tasty. Serve it with the Italian Meatballs (see page 66) instead of the polenta, with the Mushroom Ragout (see page 40), the Parsley-crusted Fish (see page 88) or with any other saucy meat, chicken or fish dish.

Mushroom, Blue Cheese and Peppadew™ Panini

Heat 15 ml oil in a large frying pan over high heat. Add half of the mushrooms, season with salt and pepper, and cook briskly for about 5 minutes until lightly browned. Remove from the pan and repeat with the rest of the mushrooms. Return all the mushrooms to the pan, stir in the chives and remove from the heat.

Brush the cut sides of the panini with olive oil and toast under a preheated grill. Rub the toasted sides with the garlic. Pile the mushrooms on the panini and arrange the blue cheese and peppadews™ on top. Place under the preheated grill until the cheese melts and starts browning. Scatter the extra chives over and serve immediately.

cook's note: Mushrooms should be cooked over high heat and in batches, to prevent them from exuding moisture. If they do become watery, keep frying over high heat until the moisture evaporates.

Instead of chopping chives, which tends to flatten and squash them, rather snip them with scissors.

±30 ml olive oil
500 g black mushrooms, thickly sliced
salt and freshly ground black pepper
50 ml snipped chives, plus extra for garnishing
3 panini (Italian bread rolls), cut in half horizontally
1 clove garlic, peeled
75 g blue cheese, thinly sliced
2 or 3 peppadews™, thinly sliced

Makes 6

A quick and tasty light lunch. Serve with rocket or watercress tossed in a piquant dressing.

Risotto Primavera

Heat 30 ml of the olive oil in a large heavy-based saucepan over medium-high heat. Add the peppers and fry for about 5 minutes until they start to soften. Stir in the asparagus and baby marrows, season lightly with salt and pepper, and stir-fry for about 3 minutes until all the vegetables are tender-crisp. Remove the vegetables from the pan and set aside.

Heat the stock in a saucepan and keep warm over low heat, barely simmering.

Place the remaining 30 ml olive oil in a large heavy-based saucepan over medium heat. Add the leeks and cook for about 10 minutes until soft but not brown. Next, add the rice and stir well for about 3 minutes, without letting it brown, until every grain of rice is coated with oil and the rice is shiny and very hot. Add the wine to the rice and simmer until absorbed, stirring continuously. Now add a ladleful of the hot stock and keep stirring until it has all been absorbed. Add the next ladleful and continue in this way for about 25 minutes until the rice grains are swollen, tender on the outside but still have a slight bite (*al dente*). The best way of testing if the rice is cooked is to taste it.

When the rice is almost cooked, stir in the cooked peppers, asparagus and baby marrows and the defrosted peas. Simmer for about 3 minutes until the peas are tender and the risotto is creamy. Add more stock if the risotto looks dry; the ideal consistency should be soft and runny, not at all solid.

Stir in the butter, Parmesan cheese, lemon rind, parsley and salt and pepper to taste. Remove from the heat, cover the pan and leave to stand for 2 minutes before serving.

cook's note: It is impossible to specify an exact amount of stock, as factors such as the size of the saucepan and the level of heat will influence the rate of evaporation and thus the amount of stock needed. You may use less or more than the specified amount.

advance preparation: Risotto is best eaten immediately, but you can reheat it in a microwave, bearing in mind that it won't be as good as when freshly cooked.

60 ml olive oil
2 small red or yellow peppers, or a mixture of the two, cut into 1 cm pieces
150 g fresh green asparagus, trimmed and cut into 2 cm pieces
3 or 4 (about 150 g) baby marrows, cut into 1 cm pieces
salt and freshly ground black pepper
±1.25 litres chicken or vegetable stock
125 g leeks, finely sliced
300 g (375 ml) arborio rice
150 ml dry white wine
110 g frozen peas, defrosted
50 g (50 ml) butter, diced
75 g (100 ml) freshly grated Parmesan cheese
finely grated rind of 1 lemon
75 ml chopped fresh Italian parsley

Serves 4 as a main course, 8 as a starter or side dish

This dish is a very good example of seasonal cooking. Primavera means spring in Italian, and risotto primavera is a basic rice dish to which springtime vegetables have been added. A properly prepared risotto requires time and tender loving care; it is not an instant dish. The lovely creamy end result makes it all worthwhile. As with all risottos, basic rules ensure a good end result: use the right kind of rice (arborio or other Italian risotto rice), do not wash the rice as this will remove the starch that makes the risotto creamy, add the liquid slowly and leave it to be absorbed before adding the next lot.
Risotto primavera is excellent as a starter, as a vegetarian main course, or as a side dish with fish or chicken.

Marmalade-baked Pork Chops
with Kumquats and Parsley Rice

4 pork chops, about 1.5 cm thick, rind trimmed off
±65 ml olive oil
65 ml orange marmalade
30 ml balsamic vinegar
10 ml chopped fresh rosemary
freshly ground black pepper
150 g (about 10) kumquats, halved around the equator
1 bunch spring onions, sliced into 3 cm pieces (include some of the green parts)
salt

You will also need:
a shallow roasting tin, lightly greased with oil or sprayed with non-stick cooking spray

Serves 4

To prevent the chops from curling as they cook, make small cuts through the fat at regular intervals.

Mix together 50 ml of the olive oil, the marmalade, vinegar, rosemary and a little freshly ground black pepper. Add the chops and turn to coat. Marinate for at least 2 hours.

Remove the chops from the marinade, reserving the marinade. Heat about 15 ml olive oil in a large frying pan over medium-high heat and sear the chops for 1 minute on each side. Place in the prepared roasting tin. Deglaze the pan with the reserved marinade, then stir in the kumquats and spring onions. Pour the sauce over the chops in the roasting tin, season the chops with salt, and roast at 180 °C for 20–30 minutes until they are cooked through, turning them over halfway through. Serve with parsley rice.

To make parsley rice:
Cook rice as usual and stir in a few tablespoons of chopped fresh Italian parsley before serving.

cook's note: To deglaze a pan means to loosen the flavourful sediment stuck to the bottom of the pan by adding liquid and stirring while it boils. The liquid can be stock, water, wine or even fruit juice, whatever is appropriate.

This is a different kind of sweet-and-sour pork that is very quick and easy to make. Marinate the chops in the morning and you will have dinner on the table in just over half an hour.
Kumquats are no longer confined to the preserving jar; they have become quite fashionable in cooking. They can be eaten with skin and all; in fact, the skin is actually sweeter than the flesh.

Parsley-crusted Fish

with Cherry Tomatoes, Asparagus and Lemon Salsa Verde

Mix together the breadcrumbs, Parmesan, parsley, lemon rind and a little salt and pepper. Stir in 45 ml of the melted butter and mix to a paste.

Place the fish in a single layer in the prepared dish. Brush with some of the remaining melted butter and season lightly with salt and pepper.

Divide the breadcrumb paste equally between the fish portions, pressing it on with your fingertips. Spoon the remaining butter over the fish. Toss the tomatoes and asparagus in the oil, season with salt and pepper and place in the dish around the fish.

Bake the fish at 200 °C for 10–15 minutes until the topping is golden brown and the fish is cooked. Quickly flash the fish under a preheated grill to get the topping nicely browned and crisp. Serve with the salsa verde.

Lemon salsa verde:

Place the parsley, mint, capers, breadcrumbs, garlic and lemon rind in a food processor and process until it forms a coarse paste. With the motor running, add the oil in a thin stream and process until smooth. Stir in the lemon juice to taste and season with salt and freshly ground black pepper.

cook's note: Kingklip or hake work well in this recipe, but you can use any fish of your choice. Make sure that all the fillets are the same thickness, or some will cook more quickly than others. It is impossible to give an exact cooking time for fish, as it depends on the thickness of the portions. Fish is cooked when it flakes easily; be careful of overcooking which will make it tough and dry.

Salsa verde, which means green sauce, has many variations, but they all include lots of herbs, hence the name.

advance preparation: The breadcrumb mixture and the salsa verde can be prepared a day in advance. Cover and refrigerate.

15 g (60 ml) fresh brown breadcrumbs
45 g (60 ml) freshly grated Parmesan cheese
60 ml chopped fresh Italian parsley
finely grated rind of 1 large lemon
salt and freshly ground black pepper
75 g (75 ml) butter, melted
650 g white fish fillets, skinned
±16 large cherry tomatoes
150 g (about 12–15) fresh green asparagus, trimmed and cut into 7 cm pieces
15 ml olive oil

For the lemon salsa verde:

175 ml fresh Italian parsley leaves, roughly chopped
100 ml fresh mint leaves, roughly chopped
30 ml capers, drained
30 g (125 ml) fresh brown breadcrumbs (about 1 slice)
2 cloves garlic, crushed
finely grated rind of 1 lemon
100 ml olive oil
±20 ml lemon juice
sea salt and freshly ground black pepper

You will also need:

a large ovenproof dish, roughly 40 x 30 cm, greased with butter

Serves 4

This dish is very quick and easy to make, yet it is good enough for entertaining. The breadcrumb topping bakes to an appealing golden brown in the oven. Serve with spring onion mashed potato (see page 83).

Mustard Chicken and Vegetable Bake

Prepare a mustard butter by mixing together the butter, mustard, oregano and freshly ground black pepper. Place in the fridge for about 15 minutes to firm up slightly.

Using your fingertips, carefully loosen the skin of each chicken thigh without detaching it from the meat, then place about 15 ml of the butter between the skin and the flesh. Carefully replace the skin and pat it into place.

Place all the vegetables in a large mixing bowl. Reserve a sprig or two of rosemary for garnishing, then add the rest to the vegetables, together with 30 ml olive oil and some salt and pepper. Toss well so that everything is coated with oil. Spread the vegetables out in the prepared roasting tray. Place the chicken thighs on top of the vegetables; brush them with the remaining olive oil and season lightly with pepper (no salt if you have used salted butter for the mustard butter). Roast at 200 °C for 45–55 minutes until the chicken is golden brown and crisp and the vegetables are cooked. Garnish with rosemary sprigs.

cook's note: It is important to use a shallow roasting tray or the veggies and chicken will steam rather than roast.

50 g (50 ml) butter, softened
30 ml grainy mustard
10 ml dried oregano
freshly ground black pepper
8 chicken thighs, trimmed of excess skin and fat
1 large onion, peeled (with the root end left intact), cut into 8 wedges
150 g baby marrows, topped and tailed and halved lengthways
1 large red or yellow pepper, quartered, seeded and cut into 3 cm strips
400 g butternut, peeled, cut into 2.5 cm pieces
about 6 sprigs fresh rosemary, plus a few extra for garnishing
±45 ml olive oil
salt

You will also need:
a large, shallow roasting tray, lightly greased

Serves 4–6

This is another one-pot meal that requires virtually no skills and very little time to prepare. Serve with a simple green salad.

Quick Mediterranean Chicken

30 ml olive oil
4 chicken breasts, skinless and deboned
salt and freshly ground black pepper
2 large cloves garlic, peeled and thinly sliced
4 plum tomatoes, roughly chopped
100 ml chicken stock
20 black or Kalamata olives, stoned and halved
15 large fresh basil leaves, shredded, plus a few extra leaves for garnishing
75 g feta cheese, crumbled

Serves 4

Heat the oil in a large frying pan over medium-high heat. Cut each chicken breast diagonally in three, season lightly with salt and pepper and fry in the oil until nicely browned. Add the garlic and stir-fry for a minute or two, then stir in the tomatoes, stock and olives.

Simmer, uncovered, for about 10 minutes until the chicken is cooked. Stir in the basil and feta, taste and add more salt and pepper if necessary. Garnish with the extra basil leaves and serve immediately.

Serve with minted couscous for a super quick-and-easy, after-work supper. For a more luxurious version, sprinkle toasted pine nuts on top.

Baby Marrow and Ricotta Cheese Tart

Top and tail the baby marrows and cut lengthways into 6 mm thick slices. Heat the olive oil in a large frying pan over medium-high heat, season the baby marrows lightly with salt and pepper and fry them for about 5 minutes until they just start to brown and soften. Set aside.

Open the pastry on a lightly floured work surface and roll into a rectangle, roughly 35 x 25 cm (it will probably be almost that size, so you will not have to do much rolling). Transfer to the baking sheet and brush the edges of the pastry with the egg yolk. Fold about 1.5 cm of the edges in towards the centre to form a border. Brush the border with the egg yolk and, with the point of a small sharp knife, draw diagonal lines on it, about 2 cm apart. Place the pastry case in the fridge for at least 30 minutes or in the freezer for 15 minutes.

Mix together the ricotta cheese, 40 g Parmesan, the whole beaten egg, chopped mint and a little freshly ground black pepper. Spread the mixture evenly over the pastry, keeping the border clear. Place the baby marrow slices on top, slightly overlapping, and scatter over the capers. Drizzle with oil and bake at 200 °C for about 20 minutes until the pastry is golden brown and well risen. Cut into squares, sprinkle over more Parmesan and garnish with mint leaves.

450 g baby marrows
15 ml olive oil, plus extra for drizzling
salt and freshly ground black pepper
400 g ready-made puff pastry, defrosted if frozen
1 egg yolk, lightly beaten with 5 ml water
200 g ricotta cheese (dried with kitchen paper if wet), crumbled
40 g (50 ml) freshly grated Parmesan cheese, plus a little bit extra for sprinkling on top
1 whole egg, lightly beaten
30 ml chopped fresh mint, plus extra leaves for garnishing
30 ml small capers, drained and dried on kitchen paper

You will also need:
a baking sheet, lightly greased

Serves 8

Ricotta, which means cooked again in Italian, is made from the whey that forms in the making of other cheeses like mozzarella or Parmesan. The cheese is relatively low in fat, making it the ideal topping in this recipe for the rather rich puff pastry. Because ricotta tastes quite bland, I have added flavour in the form of Parmesan cheese, capers and mint. The ricotta can be replaced with chunky cottage cheese, although the taste won't be quite the same.

Capers are the buds of a Mediterranean bush that are either pickled in brine or packed in salt. If you buy the ones that are packed in salt, rinse them well before use.

Serve the tart with roasted cherry tomatoes (see page 117).

Ice Cream Cake
with Coffee Fudge Sauce

For the cake:
1 litre vanilla ice cream
18 chocolate Oreo® biscuits
50 g (50 ml) butter, melted
150 g Whispers™ chocolates, roughly chopped

For the coffee fudge sauce (makes about 350 ml):
200 g sweetened condensed milk
120 g (125 ml) butter
110 g (125 ml) treacle or brown sugar
30 ml golden syrup
30 ml water
20 ml instant coffee granules

You will also need:
a 23 cm springform tin

Serves 10–12

Remove the ice cream from the freezer and leave it to soften slightly.

Process the biscuits in a food processor, add the butter and process again until well mixed. Press into the bottom of the tin and freeze while preparing the ice cream filling.

Stir the chocolates into the softened ice cream. Spread onto the biscuit crust, level the top and freeze for at least 4 hours or overnight.

About 20 minutes before serving, remove the cake from the tin and place on a serving platter. Spread over some of the sauce and let the cake stand until the ice cream is soft enough to cut. Cut into wedges with a serrated knife and serve with the rest of the sauce.

Coffee fudge sauce:
Place the condensed milk, butter, sugar, syrup and water in a saucepan over low heat and whisk constantly for about 5 minutes until everything has melted. Turn the heat up slightly and simmer gently for 2 minutes, still whisking continuously. Stir in the coffee and remove from the heat (the coffee won't dissolve completely; there will be specks left which look pretty when the sauce is spread on the cake). Leave to cool before spreading on the ice cream cake.

cook's note: Take care when making the fudge sauce – if the heat is too high and the sauce is not stirred constantly it could burn.

advance preparation: The cake can be kept in the freezer for at least a week. The sauce can be refrigerated for a week or two and can be frozen for up to two months.

This easy, make-ahead dessert looks very impressive and is always popular with adults and children alike. If you are making it for a children's birthday party, top the cake with extra Whispers™, Flake®, Smarties®, marshmallows, or whatever takes your fancy. For an adult version, scatter over some raspberries.

Chocolate Pots

with Strawberries and Almond Praline

Place the cream and chocolate in a glass bowl and place over a saucepan of simmering water. Stir until the chocolate has melted and remove from the heat.

Beat the egg yolks, sugar and cornflour for about 2 minutes until pale and creamy. Pour the cream mixture into the egg mixture, whisking constantly. Transfer to a saucepan and cook over gentle heat for about 5 minutes, stirring constantly, until the mixture thickens enough to coat the back of a spoon. Divide the mixture between the serving dishes. Leave to cool, then cover with clingfilm and refrigerate for a couple of hours or overnight.

Almond praline:
Spread out the chopped, roasted nuts on the prepared baking sheet, close together but in a single layer.

Place the sugar in a small saucepan with the water and melt over low heat while stirring. As soon as the sugar has melted, increase the heat and boil, occasionally swirling the saucepan, until the syrup turns a deep caramel brown. Immediately pour the caramel over the nuts on the baking sheet and leave until hardened.

Use a mortar and pestle or rolling pin to roughly crush the praline.

To serve:
Place the chocolate pots on six serving plates and sprinkle about ½ tablespoon of praline on each one. Top with a few sliced strawberries.

cook's note: When making the praline, do not stir the sugar once it has melted or it could crystallise.

Do not pulverise the praline when crushing it; you want to add texture to the dessert, not a layer of powder.

advance preparation: The chocolate pots can be prepared two days in advance. The praline will keep for up to two weeks in an airtight container.

For the chocolate pots:
250 ml cream
75 g dark chocolate, broken into pieces
3 egg yolks
30 g (35 ml) sugar
2.5 ml cornflour

For the almond praline:
50 g blanched almonds, roasted and roughly chopped
100 g (125 ml) sugar
100 ml water

To serve:
±300 g strawberries, sliced

You will also need:
6 small serving dishes, glass bowls or small tea cups with a capacity of 100 ml
a baking sheet, lightly oiled

Serves 6

These chocolate pots taste exquisite but they are quite rich, so serve them in small portions.
The praline provides a delightful contrast in texture to the smooth, creamy chocolate, but it can be omitted.
Leftover praline can be used to sprinkle over ice cream, or on a frosted cake.

Panna Cotta

with Lavender Biscuits and Orange-Caramel Sauce

For the panna cotta:
500 ml cream
50 g (60 ml) castor sugar
50 ml water
10 ml gelatine
10 ml vanilla essence

For the orange-caramel sauce:
125 g (150 ml) sugar
60 ml water
125 ml orange juice
5 ml grated orange rind

For the lavender biscuits (makes about 12):
100 g (175 ml) cake flour
50 g (65 ml) semolina or rice flour
50 g (60 ml) castor sugar, plus extra for sprinkling
15 ml chopped lavender petals
110 g (115 ml) butter, cut into 1.5 cm cubes and chilled
icing sugar, for dusting

You will also need:
6 dariole moulds (or other moulds of your choice), sprayed with non-stick cooking spray
a large baking sheet lined with non-stick baking paper

Serves 6

Heat the cream and sugar over low heat, stirring constantly until the sugar has dissolved. Turn up the heat and let the mixture come to boiling point, without actually letting it boil. Remove from the heat.

Meanwhile, place the water in a small bowl and sprinkle the gelatine on the water to sponge (swell). Leave for 2 minutes before adding it to the warm cream, stirring well to make sure that the gelatine is completely dissolved. Cover and leave to cool, then stir in the vanilla essence. Pour the mixture into a jug through a fine sieve and pour into the moulds. Refrigerate until set, at least 4 hours and preferably overnight.

To serve, loosen the panna cotta by running a knife around the edge or dipping the moulds briefly in hot water. Invert onto serving plates and serve with orange-caramel sauce and lavender biscuits.

Orange-caramel sauce:

Place the sugar in a small saucepan with the water and melt over low heat while stirring. As soon as the sugar has melted, increase the heat and boil, occasionally swirling the pan, until the syrup turns a deep caramel colour. Add the orange juice and stand back because the mixture will bubble vigorously. Stir over low heat to dissolve any caramel bits. Add the orange rind and cool completely.

Lavender biscuits:

Place the cake flour, semolina or rice flour, castor sugar and lavender petals in a food processor and pulse to mix. Add the butter and process until the mixture resembles fine breadcrumbs. Transfer to a lightly floured work surface and knead until the mixture comes together. Roll into a log, about 5 cm in diameter, place in a plastic bag and refrigerate for 30 minutes.

Cut 1 cm thick slices from the log and place on the prepared baking sheet. Sprinkle a little castor sugar over each biscuit and bake at 170 °C for 15–17 minutes until pale brown at the edges (the biscuits will be soft, but will harden as they cool). Cool on a wire rack. Dust with icing sugar before serving.

Panna cotta, which means cooked cream, is an Italian dessert that is very fashionable. It is extremely easy and very quick to make and you can really play around with it. It can be served with small homemade biscuits or wafers (see page 106), with fruit sauces, orange segments, fresh berries or cherries; the possibilities are endless. And if you really want to impress, serve topped with spun sugar.

The lavender biscuits are just as easy to make and you can use lavender from your garden; just make sure that it is pesticide free. The lavender can be replaced with rosemary, which is equally delicious.

cook's note: A dariole mould is a small, steep-sided cylindrical mould. If you don't have any, use ramekins or small glass bowls, or even 5 cm deep yoghurt containers.

When making the caramel sauce, do not stir the sugar once it has melted or it could crystallise.

If you are scared of turning out the panna cotta, it can be served in the dish, with a little sauce poured over the top and the biscuits served alongside. Serve the rest of the sauce separately.

advance preparation: The panna cotta can be made a day in advance. Cover and refrigerate. The sauce can be kept in the fridge for a day. The biscuits keep well for a few days in an airtight container.

special occasions

Should auld acquaintance be forgot
And never brought to mind?

Robert Burns

Alfresco Christmas Buffet

Bruschetta

with Herbed Cream Cheese and Smoked Snoek

12 slices French loaf, 1 cm thick
±45 ml olive oil
200 g creamed cottage cheese
45 ml snipped chives
30 ml chopped fresh dill, plus a few sprigs for garnishing
45 ml finely chopped peppadews™
freshly ground black pepper
±150 g smoked snoek, deboned and flaked into large pieces
lemon juice

You will also need:
a baking sheet, lightly greased

Makes 12

Brush the bread slices with olive oil on both sides, place on the baking sheet and bake at 200 °C for 5 minutes. Turn over and bake for about another 3–5 minutes until light golden brown and crisp. Remove from the oven and leave to cool.

Mix the cottage cheese with the chives, dill and peppadews™, and season with pepper. Reserve a small amount of the mixture for the topping, then spread the rest on the bruschetta. Lay a piece of snoek on each one and sprinkle with lemon juice. Place a small dollop of the cream cheese mixture on top and garnish with a small sprig of dill.

cook's note: Instead of chopping chives, which tends to flatten and squash them, rather snip them with scissors.

advance preparation: The bruschetta can be prepared a day or two in advance. Keep in an airtight container.

Serve as a starter with well-chilled, dry sparkling wine.

Stuffed Chicken Thighs
Wrapped in Bacon with Pesto Sauce

To prepare the filling, mix together the cheese, olives, pesto and herbs, and season the mixture with ground black pepper.

Open out the chicken thighs on a chopping board and season lightly with salt and pepper. Place about 15 ml of the filling in the centre of each thigh. Roll up and wrap each thigh in a rasher of bacon. Thread two wrapped thighs onto each skewer with one bay leaf in between. Place in a single layer in the prepared pan.

Drizzle with olive oil and grind over a little black pepper. Bake at 200 °C for about 25 minutes until the chicken is cooked through and the bacon is crisp, turning them over halfway through. Transfer to a serving dish, making sure that you scrape out all the sauce and cheesy bits that may be stuck to the pan. Sprinkle over any leftover filling and serve immediately with the sauce passed separately.

Sun-dried tomato pesto:
Process the pine nuts, tomatoes, Parmesan, garlic and basil in a food processor until a coarse paste is formed. With the motor running, add the oil in a steady stream and process until evenly blended. Taste and add salt and pepper if necessary.

Sauce:
Place the pesto, tomato paste and about 50 ml of stock in a small saucepan and whisk to combine. Add just enough of the remaining stock to make a sauce with a thick pouring consistency. Season with salt and pepper, and heat over low heat.

cook's note: If necessary, place the chicken under a pre-heated grill for a minute or two to get the bacon really crisp.

advance preparation: Prepare the filling and sauce a day in advance. The chicken can be prepared early in the day, ready to be baked. Cover with clingfilm and refrigerate.

125 g goat's or feta cheese, grated or crumbled
15 black olives, stoned and roughly chopped
50 ml sun-dried tomato pesto (see below)
25 ml chopped fresh rosemary
25 ml fresh thyme leaves
salt and freshly ground black pepper
16 large, deboned chicken thighs
±350 g streaky bacon
8 bay leaves
olive oil

For the sun-dried tomato pesto (makes ±250 ml):
50 g (100 ml) pine nuts, toasted
50 g sun-dried tomatoes in oil, well drained and roughly chopped
40 g (50 ml) freshly grated Parmesan cheese
2 cloves garlic
handful of fresh basil leaves (about 100 ml, packed)
100 ml olive oil
salt and freshly ground black pepper

For the sauce (makes ±500 ml):
120 ml sun-dried tomato pesto
60 ml tomato paste
±400 ml chicken stock
salt and freshly ground black pepper

You will also need:
8 wooden skewers
a shallow, greased oven pan

Makes 8 skewers

This recipe is a breeze to put together if you can get hold of deboned chicken thighs. However, if these are not available, bone the thighs yourself. Use a semi-hard goat's cheese for the filling, such as Gotino from Fairview.

Salmon Cheesecake

200 g cream crackers
125 g (130 ml) butter, melted
15 ml olive oil
1 bunch spring onions, chopped (include some of the green parts)
500 g creamed cottage cheese, at room temperature
4 eggs
250 ml sour cream
1 x 415 g can salmon, well drained (or 2 x 170 g cans tuna in water, well drained and flaked)
50 ml chopped fresh dill, plus extra for garnishing
finely grated rind of 1 large lemon
15 ml lemon juice
1.25 ml cayenne pepper
salt and freshly ground black pepper
a few pink peppercorns, to garnish (optional)

You will also need:
a 23 cm springform tin, sprayed with non-stick cooking spray and base-lined with non-stick baking paper

Makes 10–12 slices

Although it takes a bit of time to prepare, the cheesecake tastes terrific and looks so pretty on a buffet table that it is well worth the effort. To make it even more special, drape a piece of smoked salmon over each slice. Pink peppercorns are not really peppercorns but are, in fact, the pungent berries of a South American poison ivy. They are not hot, just slightly aromatic, and are used more for their looks than their taste. Use in sauces, with fish or poultry, or as a garnish.

Process the crackers in a food processor, add the melted butter and process again until well mixed. Press firmly into the bottom of the prepared tin. Refrigerate while you prepare the filling.

Heat the oil in a frying pan and cook the spring onions over low heat for about 5 minutes until soft but not brown.

Place the cottage cheese in a large bowl and whisk the eggs in one by one. Add half of the sour cream (125 ml) and whisk until everything is well mixed.

Remove the skins, if any, from the salmon and flake the flesh. Stir into the cottage cheese mixture, together with the cooked spring onions, dill, lemon rind, lemon juice and cayenne pepper. Season the mixture with salt and pepper to taste. Spoon onto the prepared crust and bake at 180 °C for 50–60 minutes until golden brown on top and just set.

Run a knife along the side of the tin to prevent the cheesecake from cracking, then leave to cool in the tin for 1 hour. Release the cake from the tin. Leave it to cool completely, then place on a large serving platter. Spread the remaining sour cream on top of the cake and cut it into 10 or 12 slices.

Crush the peppercorns in a mortar or with a rolling pin, and sprinkle a little bit on each slice of cheesecake. Top each slice with a sprig of dill.

cook's note: Do not be concerned if the cheesecake cracks a little; the sour cream topping will conceal it. If the cheesecake browns too much while baking, cover it lightly with foil.

Bake the cheesecake just until set and no longer, as it will keep on cooking a little bit after being removed from the oven.

advance preparation: The cheesecake can be prepared at least a day in advance. Keep refrigerated, but serve at room temperature, not ice cold.

Roast Fillet of Beef
with Asparagus, Balsamic Onions and Chimichurri Sauce

Mix together the peppercorns, herbs and brown sugar. Tie the fillet with kitchen string to keep it in a neat shape. Season the meat with salt and spread with the mustard. Press the peppercorn mixture onto the surface of the meat, coating it evenly.

Heat the olive oil in a frying pan and brown the meat well on all sides. Place the meat on a rimmed baking sheet and roast at 220 °C until done to your liking, about 20 minutes for medium-rare.

If serving it hot, leave it to rest for about 15 minutes before carving. If serving at room temperature, leave it to cool completely, then cover and carve just before serving.

Cut the fillet against the grain into 5 mm thick slices. Arrange overlapping meat slices on a large serving platter with the asparagus on either side. Spoon a thin ribbon of the sauce down the centre of the meat. Garnish with the extra thyme sprigs and serve the onions and the rest of the sauce on the side.

Asparagus:
Place the asparagus in a large mixing bowl. Add the oil and salt and pepper, and toss to coat. Roast at 200 °C for about 10 minutes until tender-crisp. Serve hot or at room temperature.

Balsamic onions:
Heat the oil in a large frying pan over medium-low heat, add the onions and cook gently for about 10 minutes until they start to brown. Add the vinegar, stock, sugar, thyme and salt and pepper. Cover the pan and cook the onions over low heat for about 30 minutes until tender, stirring occasionally. Add a little more stock if it looks dry. Sprinkle the extra thyme leaves on top. Serve hot or at room temperature.

Chimichurri sauce:
Mix together the herbs, olive oil, chilli sauce, vinegar, garlic and crushed chillies, and season the sauce with salt and pepper. Serve at room temperature.

20 ml black peppercorns, coarsely crushed
50 ml fresh thyme leaves, chopped, plus a few extra sprigs for garnishing
15 ml chopped fresh rosemary
10 ml brown sugar
1.25 kg fillet of beef, well trimmed of fat and sinew
salt
25 ml Dijon mustard
±15 ml olive oil

For the asparagus:
300 g fresh green asparagus, trimmed
30 ml olive oil
salt and freshly ground black pepper

For the balsamic onions:
60 ml olive oil
600 g pickling onions, peeled
75 ml balsamic vinegar
50 ml beef stock
15 ml brown sugar
15 ml fresh thyme leaves, plus extra for sprinkling on top
salt and freshly ground black pepper

For the chimichurri sauce (makes about 200 ml):
350 ml (firmly packed) fresh Italian parsley leaves, finely chopped
150 ml (firmly packed) fresh coriander leaves, finely chopped
100 ml olive oil
30 ml sweet chilli sauce
20 ml red wine vinegar
3 cloves garlic, crushed
2.5 ml crushed chillies
Maldon® sea salt
freshly ground black pepper

You will also need:
kitchen string
a rimmed baking tray

Serves 8

cook's note: Beef fillet is best served medium-rare or medium. Cooking time will depend on the size and shape of the fillet; a long thin piece of meat will obviously need less time to cook than a fat, round piece of the same weight. Also bear in mind that the meat will still carry on cooking once it has been removed from the oven.

Pickling onions are easier to peel if you blanch them first.

advance preparation: The beef can be cooked a day in advance and can also be frozen. Leave it to cool, wrap it in foil and freeze. Defrost overnight in the fridge. Leave it to reach room temperature and slice just before serving. The onions can be cooked a day in advance.

The beauty of this dish is that it can be served hot or at room temperature, which means that you can prepare it all in advance if you choose to serve it at room temperature. Chimichurri is an Argentine parsley sauce that goes well with any roast beef. It is actually more like a condiment than a sauce, so you don't need a large quantity of it. To retain the bright green colour of the sauce, do not make it too far in advance.

Cracked Paprika Potatoes

900 g potatoes
±60 ml olive oil
salt and freshly ground black pepper
±2.5 ml paprika

You will also need:
a large, shallow ovenproof dish, brushed with olive oil

Serves 8

Boil whole, unpeeled potatoes until tender. Drain well, place on a chopping board and bash with a rolling pin to crack. Place the potatoes in the prepared dish and drizzle with olive oil. Season with salt and pepper and sprinkle with paprika. Bake at 230 °C for 35–40 minutes until crisp and golden brown.

advance preparation: The potatoes can be cooked, bashed and placed in the oven dish, ready to be baked, a few hours in advance.

Coffee Ice Cream Bombes
with Crushed Raspberries and Macadamia Nut Wafers

Place the condensed milk in a bowl and stir in the dissolved coffee. Place the cream in a large mixing bowl and, using an electric whisk, beat till softly peaking. Whisk the condensed milk mixture into the cream until well blended and thick.

In a clean glass bowl and using clean beaters, whisk the egg whites with a pinch of salt until firm but not quite stiff and fold into the cream mixture. Pour the ice cream into the moulds and place in the freezer overnight. Freeze leftover ice cream in another container, or use more moulds.

Macadamia nut wafers:
Place the sugar, syrup and butter in a small saucepan and stir over low heat for about 6 minutes until smooth. Do not let it boil. Remove from the heat and stir in the flour and nuts.

Place teaspoonfuls of the mixture about 6 cm apart on the prepared baking sheets. Bake at 190 °C for 5–8 minutes until golden brown. Remove from the oven and let the wafers cool and harden for about 5 minutes before transferring to a wire rack. Store in an airtight container when cold.

For the ice cream (makes about 1.6 litres):

1 x 397 g can sweetened condensed milk
60 ml instant coffee, dissolved in 30 ml boiling water
500 ml cream
2 egg whites

For the macadamia nut wafers (makes about 18):

45 g (50 ml) brown sugar
45 ml golden syrup
30 g (30 ml) butter
20 g (35 ml) cake flour
35 g macadamia nuts, finely chopped

To serve:
300 g fresh raspberries
±35 g (±45 ml) castor sugar
fresh mint leaves, to decorate

You will also need:
8 x dariole moulds, or other moulds with a capacity of 175 ml
2 baking sheets lined with non-stick baking paper

Serves 8

To serve:
Place the raspberries in a mixing bowl and lightly crush with a fork. Stir in the sugar, taste, and add more sugar if necessary.

To turn out the ice cream bombes, run a knife around the ice cream and invert onto serving plates. Place a large spoonful of raspberries on each one, letting some tumble off onto the plate. Decorate with mint and serve with the macadamia nut wafers.

cook's note: Dariole moulds are small, steep-sided cylindrical moulds made of metal, used for making puddings, cakes or pastries.

Work quickly when unmoulding and serving the ice cream, as it melts quicker than commercial ice creams.

If the wafer mixture becomes too hard to handle, reheat briefly before continuing.

advance preparation: The ice cream tastes best if freshly made but it can be kept in the freezer for up to a week. Cover the moulds with clingfilm. The wafers will keep for at least a week in an airtight container.

The coffee ice cream is superb; it tastes smooth and velvety without having to be churned, so you don't even need an ice cream machine to make it. The macadamia nut wafers are really quick and easy to make, too, and very yummy. Another option for a delicious dessert is to freeze store-bought ice cream in a loaf tin and serve it in thick slices with the wafers and the coffee fudge sauce (see page 93). I use dariole moulds in which to freeze the ice cream, but you can use any mould with a capacity of at least 175 ml.

New Year's Eve Drinks Party

Allow 6–10 snacks per person for a cocktail party. Select hot and cold snacks, and include at least one item that is suitable for vegetarians.

Other ideas for the menu: chilled pea and lettuce soup (see page 12) served in small glasses with straws; tuna and avocado melts (see page 56); caramelised onion, asparagus and gruyère tartlets (see page 78).

Smoked Salmon and Trout Phyllo Tartlets

For the phyllo pastry cases:

±6 sheets of phyllo pastry
±100 g (±100 ml) butter, melted

For the filling:

250 g smoked trout fillets, skinned and flaked
50 g (±500 ml) watercress, roughly chopped, plus extra for garnishing
30 ml mayonnaise
60 ml creamed horseradish
±12 chives, snipped
finely grated rind of 1 lemon
1 large avocado, cut into 1 cm pieces, plus extra for garnishing
lemon juice
salt and freshly ground black pepper
100 g thinly sliced smoked salmon, cut into slivers

You will also need:

2 x 12-cup patty pan trays, the cups 6 cm wide and 2 cm deep, brushed with some of the melted butter
a 9 cm cookie cutter

Makes 20

Brush 3 sheets of phyllo pastry with butter and place on top of one another. Cut out rounds with the cookie cutter and line the prepared cups with the pastry (the filling is sufficient for about 20, so line just 20 of the cups). Bake the pastry cases at 190 °C for about 8 minutes until golden brown. Transfer to a wire rack to cool.

Filling:

In a large bowl lightly mix together the trout, watercress, mayonnaise, horseradish, chives, and lemon rind. Fold in the avocado. Add the lemon juice, and salt and pepper to taste.

Carefully spoon some of the mixture into each baked phyllo case. Drape a few slivers of smoked salmon on top and garnish with avocado and watercress.

cook's note: Keep the phyllo sheets you are not working with covered with a damp tea towel to prevent them from drying out.

advance preparation: The pastry cases can be baked a few days in advance. Keep in an airtight container. The filling can be prepared up to 6 hours in advance. Fill the cases shortly before serving.

The ideal partner for well-chilled, dry sparkling wine.

Cheesy Pesto Puffs

Open out the pastry on a lightly floured work surface and roll out until about 3 mm thick. Stamp out rounds with the cookie cutter and place on the baking sheet. Spread each round with pesto and top with 2 slices of cherry tomato. Season lightly with salt and pepper, and place a few pieces of pecorino cheese on top.

Refrigerate for at least 30 minutes, then bake at 200 °C until well-risen and golden brown, about 15 minutes. Serve hot, garnished with thyme or rosemary.

advance preparation: The rounds can be cut out, spread with pesto and refrigerated for up to one day. Finish them the next day, refrigerate again for at least 30 minutes and bake just before serving.

400 g ready-made puff pastry, defrosted if frozen
±160 ml sun-dried tomato pesto (see page 102) or store-bought pesto
±18 small cherry tomatoes, thinly sliced
salt and freshly ground black pepper
±60 g pecorino cheese, shaved or thinly sliced
fresh thyme or rosemary sprigs, to garnish

You will also need:
a 5 cm cookie cutter
a baking sheet, lightly greased

Makes about 32

These appetising bites can be put together in no time at all and provide a lovely vegetarian option. The pecorino cheese can be replaced with mature Cheddar.

Bruschetta
with Goat's Cheese and Pepper and Olive Salsa

To make the bruschetta, cut the bread diagonally into 1 cm thick slices. Continue until you have 20 slices. Brush the bread with olive oil on both sides, place on the baking sheet and bake at 200 °C for 5 minutes. Turn over and bake for a further 3–5 minutes until light golden brown and crisp. Rub the bread with the garlic on one side, and leave to cool.

Spread each bruschetta with goat's cheese and top with some of the salsa, pureéd if preferred.

advance preparation: The bruschetta can be stored in an airtight container for at least two days.

1 French loaf
±75 ml olive oil
1 or 2 cloves garlic, peeled
±250 g soft goat's cheese
1 quantity roasted pepper and olive salsa (see page 124)

You will also need:
a baking sheet, lightly greased

Makes 20

Mini Toad-in-the-hole Muffins

120 g (215 ml) cake flour
250 ml milk
2 eggs
2.5 ml salt
10 ml grainy mustard
15 ml chopped fresh thyme
±75 ml sunflower oil
±200 g thin sausage, cut into 2 cm pieces
chutney of your choice, to serve

You will also need:
2 x 12-cup mini muffin trays, either non-stick or sprayed with non-stick cooking spray

Makes about 30

Blend the flour, milk, eggs and salt together in a blender until smooth. Stir in the mustard and thyme, pour into a jug, cover and refrigerate for 1 hour.

Preheat the oven to 220 °C. Pour 2.5 ml oil into each of the muffin cups and place the trays in the oven for about 5 minutes until the oil is very hot, almost smoking. Remove the trays from the oven and quickly place a piece of sausage in each cup. Pour some batter in each cup, filling them almost to the top. Bake for 12–15 minutes until puffed up and golden brown. Remove from the trays and keep warm while baking more muffins with the remaining batter and sausage. Once removed from the oven the muffins will sink in the centre, while the edges will stay puffy.

To serve, place a dollop of chutney on each muffin.

cook's note: If making the batter by hand, whisk together the flour and eggs, then gradually add the milk. Stir in the mustard, thyme and salt. If lumps occur, pour the batter through a sieve.

advance preparation: The muffins can be prepared a day in advance. Refrigerate overnight and reheat at 180 °C for 5–10 minutes.

These look very cute and are easy to make. Use a good-quality, thin sausage, preferably boerewors, and try to avoid very fatty types, like lamb sausage.

Picadillo Empanadas

Cut 1 cm thick rounds from the pastry log and place on a lightly floured work surface. Roll the rounds out until about 3 mm thick, cut a 9 cm circle out of each one with a cookie cutter and place on the prepared baking sheet. You can gather the off-cuts and roll them again to make more circles if you wish.

Brush the edges of the circles with beaten egg yolk. Place about a tablespoon of picadillo in the centre of each circle and fold in half to enclose the filling, forming half-moons. Press the edges together firmly and use a fork to seal them well. Brush with egg yolk, sprinkle over some poppy seeds and refrigerate for at least 30 minutes. Bake at 200 °C for about 20 minutes until golden brown.

cook's note: There will be some picadillo left over which you can save for another use.

advance preparation: The finished empanadas can be frozen. Bake from frozen, but allow some extra time.

1 quantity rich shortcrust pastry (see page 58), the dough formed into a 6 cm thick log, not into a disc
1 egg yolk, lightly beaten with a few drops of water
1 quantity picadillo (see page 122)
poppy seeds, for sprinkling

You will also need:
a 9 cm cookie cutter
a large baking sheet, sprayed with non-stick cooking spray

Makes about 20

Empanadas are small pies served in tapas bars all over Spain. They can be filled with spinach and feta, roast chicken or butternut. The picadillo filling is always popular.

Strawberry Macaroons

For the macaroons:
3 egg whites
pinch of salt
100 g (125 ml) castor sugar
65 g (200 ml) desiccated coconut
40 g (100 ml) cocoa powder, sifted
100 g dark chocolate, roughly chopped

For serving:
strawberries, preferably small ones, stems intact
cocoa powder, for dusting
±100 ml crème fraîche

You will also need:
2 large baking sheets lined with non-stick baking paper

Makes about 35

Place the egg whites in a large bowl with a pinch of salt and whisk until stiff peaks form. Start whisking in the sugar, a tablespoon at a time, whisking well after each addition. Continue whisking until the egg whites are stiff and glossy. Stir in the coconut, cocoa and chocolate and mix well.

Spoon heaped teaspoonfuls (about 10 ml) of the mixture onto the prepared baking sheets, spacing them a few centimetres apart. With the back of a teaspoon flatten them slightly, into 3.5 cm rounds. Place in a 180 °C oven, turn off the oven and leave to dry out overnight.

To assemble, slice the strawberries if large. Dust the macaroons with cocoa powder and place a small dollop of crème fraîche on each one. Top with a small whole strawberry or a strawberry slice.

cook's note: Do not flatten the macaroons too much when spooning them onto the baking sheet; they taste better if they are quite chunky, rather than flat.

advance preparation: The macaroons can be prepared at least a week in advance. Store in an airtight container.

Crunchy and light, these morsels can be whipped up in minutes and they taste great, even without the topping.

Fudge Tartlets

with Chocolate and Hazelnut Topping

For the sweet shortcrust pastry:
180 g (325 ml) cake flour
45 g (75 ml) icing sugar
large pinch of salt
120 g (125 ml) butter, cut into 1.5 cm cubes and chilled
1 egg
cold water, if necessary

For the fudge:
200 g (150 ml) sweetened condensed milk
120 g (125 ml) butter
120 g (140 ml) brown sugar
30 ml golden syrup
30 ml whisky (optional)

Place the flour, icing sugar and salt in a food processor and pulse to mix. Add the butter and process again until the mixture resembles fine breadcrumbs. Add the egg and process just until the mixture comes together. Add water only if necessary. Form the dough into a log, about 4 cm in diameter, place in a plastic bag and refrigerate for 30 minutes.

The easiest way to bake the tartlet shells is by lining one tray with dough and lightly pressing another (empty) tray into the lined tin. This eliminates the need for blind baking, and ensures that the shells keep their shape. If you have 4 tins, proceed as follows, otherwise you will have to do it in two batches.

Using a serrated knife, cut the dough log into 5 mm thick rounds; you should have about 24. Press the rounds evenly into the tins, then neatly trim off the excess with a sharp knife. Freeze the tartlet shells for 15 minutes.

Prick each shell lightly with a cocktail stick. Lightly press the empty trays into the lined ones and bake at 190 °C for 10 minutes. Remove the top trays and bake for about another 2–3 minutes until the pastry is cooked through and the edges are lightly browned.

Leave the tartlet shells to cool completely.

Fudge:

Place the condensed milk, butter, sugar and syrup in a saucepan over low heat and whisk constantly until everything is melted. Simmer gently for about 5 minutes, stirring continuously, until thick. Remove from the heat and stir in the whisky.

For the chocolate and hazelnut topping:
60 g dark chocolate, melted
±20 g hazelnuts (you need 24), roasted and rubbed in a clean tea towel to remove the skins

You will also need:
at least 2 x 12-cup mini muffin trays, but preferably 4

Makes 24

Assembling the tartlets:
Using a teaspoon, fill the shells right to the top with fudge. Leave to set, then pour a dollop of chocolate onto each tartlet and place a hazelnut in the middle.

cook's note: Take care when making the fudge; if the heat is too high and you don't stir constantly, it could burn.

advance preparation: The pastry can be kept in the fridge for a day or two. The baked shells will keep for a few days in an airtight container. The fudge can be kept in the fridge for a few days; bring it to room temperature or flash it in the microwave before filling the shells. The fudge can also be frozen. The assembled tartlets keep well in the fridge for at least three days.

These dainty tartlets are just a mouthful of sweet indulgence. You will probably have some fudge left over, but I can guarantee that you won't have a problem getting rid of it. Reheat over low heat, add a wee bit more whisky, and pour over ice cream. Yum!

Book Club Brunch

Fresh Dates and Oranges

with Greek Yoghurt and Toasted Sunflower Seeds

8 fresh dates, pitted and sliced
4 oranges, segmented
Greek yoghurt, to serve
30 ml sunflower seeds, toasted

Serves 4

Mix together the dates and oranges, spoon into serving dishes and top with a dollop of Greek yoghurt. Sprinkle the sunflower seeds on top.

cook's note: To segment an orange, cut off both ends and place the orange upright on a chopping board. Working from top to bottom and using a serrated knife, cut off the peel and pith in narrow strips. Now hold the orange in your hand and cut along both sides of each segment, between the fruit and the membrane, to release each segment.

A healthy and refreshing starter or dessert. If you can get hold of them, use navel oranges, which are mostly seedless.

Roasted Cherry Tomatoes

350 g cherry tomatoes
30 ml olive oil
5 ml balsamic vinegar
freshly ground black pepper
5 ml brown sugar
sea salt
small handful of fresh mint or oregano leaves

You will also need:
a shallow ovenproof dish

Serves 6

Place the cherry tomatoes in the ovenproof dish, add the olive oil, balsamic vinegar and some pepper, and toss to coat. Sprinkle over the brown sugar and roast at 200 °C for about 10 minutes until the tomatoes start to wrinkle and burst. Season the tomatoes with sea salt and sprinkle the mint or oregano leaves on top.

Bacon-wrapped Sausages
with Onion Marmalade

Make a lengthways incision in each sausage without cutting all the way through. Cut the cheese into sticks that will fit into the incision. Fill the incisions with the sticks of cheese and press together to close. Wrap each sausage in a rasher or two of bacon. Press a wooden skewer lengthways through each sausage to create a 'lolly'.

Grill or char grill the sausages for about 10 minutes until the bacon is crisp and the cheese starts melting, giving them a turn every now and then.

Serve with mustard and onion marmalade.

Onion marmalade:
Place the oil in a large frying pan over low heat, add the onions and cook for about 30 minutes until soft but not brown, stirring occasionally. Add the sugar, vinegar and orange juice, and stir constantly until the sugar has melted. Simmer, uncovered, for about 30 minutes until thickened, stirring frequently. Stir in the thyme and season with salt and pepper.

cook's note: It may seem like a lot of onions, but they shrink remarkably.

advance preparation: The sausages can be prepared, ready for cooking, a day in advance. The onion marmalade will keep in the fridge for a week or two.

4 sausages, each about 40–50 g
±60 g gruyère cheese
4–8 rashers rindless, smoked, streaky bacon
mustard, to serve

For the onion marmalade:
45 ml olive oil
750 g onions, thinly sliced
200 g (235 ml) treacle or brown sugar
60 ml balsamic vinegar
30 ml orange juice
5 ml fresh thyme leaves
salt and freshly ground black pepper

You will also need:
8 wooden skewers

Makes 4

For this dish you need sausages that do not require any cooking, such as bockwurst, country sausage or frankfurters.
It is difficult to specify an exact quantity for the cheese and bacon, as it will depend on the thickness and length of the sausage. The gruyère cheese can be replaced with mature Cheddar.
Leftover onion marmalade is delicious in a cheese sandwich or served as part of a cheese platter.

Broccoli and Feta Frittata

30 ml olive oil
175 g broccoli florets
salt
7 eggs
50 ml milk
100 g feta cheese, crumbled
freshly ground black pepper

You will also need:
a 25 cm heavy-based, non-stick frying pan

Serves 4 as a light main course

Heat the oil in the pan over medium-high heat and stir-fry the broccoli for about 5 minutes until tender-crisp. Season the broccoli very lightly with salt.

Whisk together the eggs, milk and half of the feta, and season the mixture with pepper (no salt because the feta is salty enough). Pour the mixture over the broccoli in the pan and cook over low heat, without stirring, for 7–12 minutes until lightly browned underneath and almost set on top.

Sprinkle over the remaining feta cheese and place under a preheated grill for about 2 minutes to lightly brown the cheese and set the top. Cut into wedges to serve.

advance preparation: The frittata can be made a day ahead. Cover and refrigerate. Serve at room temperature.

A frittata is a thick Italian omelette, cooked slowly over low heat. It can be served warm or at room temperature and is ideal for taking on a picnic.

Latin American Birthday Feast

This menu is great for entertaining as everything, except the chicken, can be prepared in advance. While the chicken is being cooked, serve the soup as a starter. For the main course, place the cooked chicken on a serving table together with the picadillo, pancakes and salsas. Add a bowl of sour cream and some salad leaves. Invite your guests to roll their own pancakes with whatever filling they fancy. End on a sweet and spicy note with the chocolate-chilli ice cream with nectarines. If nectarines are not in season, replace with chunky wedges of pineapple.

Tortilla Soup

8 plum tomatoes, halved
45 ml olive oil
5 ml brown sugar
salt and freshly ground black pepper
1 onion, finely chopped
2 cloves garlic, crushed
1 or 2 red chillies (depending on the strength), seeds removed and finely chopped
1 x 400 g can chopped tomatoes
900 ml chicken stock
10 ml ground cumin
75 g corn (tortilla) chips
100 ml chopped fresh Italian parsley
±60 ml sour cream

You will also need:
a shallow roasting tin

Serves 6

In New Mexico, where this dish is a speciality, the soup is thickened with fried tortillas. My version contains corn chips for thickening, making it much quicker and easier. If this soup is not part of the menu, add diced avocado, grated cheese and strips of grilled chicken for a complete meal.

Arrange the tomatoes, cut side up, in a shallow roasting tin. Drizzle with 15 ml olive oil, sprinkle with brown sugar and season with salt and pepper. Roast at 220 °C for about 25 minutes until the tomatoes start turning brown at the edges.

Meanwhile, heat the remaining 30 ml oil in a large frying pan, add the onion and cook for about 10 minutes until softened. Add the garlic and chillies and stir-fry for another minute or two.

Briefly process or roughly chop the roasted tomatoes and add, with their juices, to the onions in the pan. Stir in the canned tomatoes, stock and cumin. Reserve a few of the corn chips for garnishing, then roughly crush the rest and stir into the soup. Cover the soup and simmer for 20 minutes. Stir in the parsley, salt and pepper to taste and more stock or water if the soup is too thick. Spoon into serving bowls and top each one with a dollop of sour cream and a corn chip or two.

cook's note: Roasting the tomatoes really intensifies their flavour, so don't be tempted to skip this step.

Take care when handling fresh chillies, as they contain a substance called capsaicin that can burn your skin. Wear gloves when preparing them or thoroughly wash your hands afterwards.

advance preparation: The soup can be prepared a day in advance.

Picadillo

Place about 30 ml oil in a large frying pan over medium-low heat, add the onion and cook for about 10 minutes until soft and translucent. Add the garlic and stir-fry for another minute or two. Remove the onion mixture from the pan and reserve.

Add a little more oil to the pan and turn up the heat. Working in batches, brown the meat in the pan, breaking up clumps with a fork. Return all the meat to the pan and stir in the reserved onion mixture, the tomatoes, stock, tomato paste, cumin, oregano, chilli powder or crushed chillies, sugar and salt and pepper. Cover the pan and simmer over low heat for 1 hour, adding more stock or water if the mixture gets too dry.

Stir in the parsley, then taste and add more salt and pepper if necessary.

cook's note: For the best flavour, use Italian canned tomatoes.

advance preparation: Picadillo can be prepared a day in advance and can also be frozen.

±45 ml sunflower oil
1 large onion, finely chopped
2 cloves garlic, crushed
500 g minced beef
1 x 400 g can chopped tomatoes
200 ml beef stock
15 ml tomato paste
10 ml ground cumin
10 ml dried oregano
a pinch of chilli powder or crushed chillies
2.5 ml sugar
salt and freshly ground black pepper
100 ml chopped fresh Italian parsley

Serves 6

Picadillo, a spicy mince mixture, is a favourite dish in many Latin American countries. It has many variations but the basic ingredients are usually minced meat and tomatoes. Picadillo is very versatile, and can be served with rice, pasta or mashed potato; on a hamburger bun; in taco shells or tortillas; as a topping for baked potato or as a stuffing for halved roasted butternuts. To make the mince mixture go further, add a can of drained black or kidney beans.

Spicy Chicken

20 ml chopped fresh thyme
or 10 ml dried thyme
12.5 ml paprika
10 ml dried oregano
5 ml coarsely ground black pepper
5 ml cayenne pepper
5 ml mustard powder
5 ml salt
8 chicken breasts, skinless and deboned
±30 ml olive oil

Serves 6

A healthy, low-fat way to prepare chicken breasts. However, be careful of overcooking as this will make the chicken tough and dry.

Make the spice mix by mixing together the thyme, paprika, oregano, black and cayenne pepper, mustard powder and salt.

Brush the chicken breasts with olive oil on both sides, then coat with the spice mix, pressing it on with your fingertips. Char grill or braai/barbecue the chicken breasts until crisp on the outside and just cooked through but still moist inside. To serve, cut the chicken into strips.

cook's note: To oven bake the chicken, place on a greased baking sheet and bake at 200 °C for about 20 minutes until just cooked through.

advance preparation: The spice mix will keep for a couple of days in an airtight container.

Polenta Pancakes

100 g (175 ml) cake flour
100 g (140 ml) polenta
2.5 ml salt
2 eggs
350 ml milk
45 ml sunflower oil

You will also need:
a 22 cm (inside base measurement) non-stick frying pan

Makes about 12

It takes practice to get these pancakes quite thin, so don't despair if you have to discard the first one or two! You can use ready-made tortillas, but they are expensive and not as tasty as home-made polenta pancakes.

Sift the flour, polenta and salt together. Whisk the eggs, milk and oil together until well blended. Add the egg mixture to the dry ingredients and whisk until smooth. Pour into a large jug, cover and leave to stand for at least 30 minutes.

Wipe the pan with a piece of kitchen paper dipped in oil and place over medium heat. As soon as the pan is hot, pour in about 65 ml of the batter, swirling the pan to spread it evenly over the bottom. Cook until bubbles form on the surface and the pancake is lightly browned underneath. Flip it over with a palette knife and cook until lightly browned on the other side. Transfer to a plate and repeat with the rest of the batter.

cook's note: Stir the mixture well before baking each pancake to ensure an even distribution of the polenta.

advance preparation: The batter can be made a day in advance. The pancakes can be cooked a day in advance and can also be frozen, interleaved with pieces of greaseproof paper and wrapped in foil. Leave to defrost and heat in the foil at 180 °C for about 10 minutes.

Salsas

Fresh Corn and Avocado Salsa

Place the avocado in a bowl, add some lemon juice and toss gently to mix. Cut the corn kernels off the cob and stir into the avocado, together with the onion, chilli and coriander. Season with salt and pepper just before serving.

1 avocado, cut into 1.5 cm pieces
lemon juice
1 fresh raw sweet corn cob
½ small red onion or 3 spring onions, finely chopped
1 small red chilli, seeded and finely chopped (optional)
50 ml chopped fresh coriander
sea salt and freshly ground black pepper

Serves 6

Roasted Pepper and Olive Salsa

Mix together the peppers, olives, oil and parsley and season with salt and pepper to taste.

Leave to stand for at least 30 minutes before serving.

1 small red and 1 small yellow or orange pepper, roasted, peeled and cut into 1 cm pieces (see page 9)
60 g black olives, stoned and sliced
10 ml olive oil
50 ml roughly chopped fresh Italian parsley
sea salt and freshly ground black pepper

Serves 6

The word salsa means sauce in Spanish. Salsas originated in Mexico but are now popular worldwide. They consist of chopped vegetables and/or fruit and are generally quite healthy. Both salsas can be prepared up to four hours in advance.

White Chocolate-Chilli Ice Cream

with Caramelised Nectarines

For the ice cream:
1 litre vanilla ice cream, slightly softened
150 g white chocolate, coarsely grated
2 or 3 fresh red chillies (depending on the strength), seeded and finely chopped

For the caramelised nectarines:
6–8 nectarines, stoned and thickly sliced
±100 g (±125 ml) sugar
fresh mint leaves, to decorate

You will also need:
a 22 x 12 cm loaf tin, 7 cm deep, lined with clingfilm
a non-stick frying pan

Serves 8

Mix the ice cream, chocolate and chillies together well and spoon the mixture into the prepared tin. Freeze for at least 6 hours or overnight. Remove from the freezer 20 minutes before serving.

Unmould the ice cream and peel off the clingfilm. With a serrated knife, cut the ice cream into thick slices and serve with the nectarines.

Nectarines:
Place the non-stick frying pan over high heat until very hot. Press the nectarines in the sugar, coating them thoroughly. Add to the hot pan and fry until caramelised, turning over after about half a minute. Decorate with mint and serve immediately.

cook's note: Keep a constant watch over the nectarines while they are caramelising as they burn very easily.

Plain vanilla ice cream gets a makeover with white chocolate and chilli. This is the cheat's way of doing it, using store-bought ice cream. If you have an ice-cream maker, make a basic vanilla ice cream, infusing the cream with the chilli and stirring in the chocolate before churning. Don't let the chilli in the ice cream put you off; it just adds a touch of spiciness, which works really well with the sweetness of the fruit.
Any ice cream looks much more stylish if it is served in slices rather than scooped from a tub, therefore I refreeze the ice cream in a loaf tin. However, if preferred, you can simply spoon it back into the ice cream container for freezing.
If nectarines are not available, replace with plums, pineapple, mangoes or pears.

Suggested Menus

I know it sounds like a cliché, but less really is more these days when it comes to entertaining. It is not necessary to serve a three-course meal. In fact, I think that guests enjoy the main course more if there is not a starter. So definitely think about serving only one or two courses.

Summer:

Bruschetta with goat's cheese and pepper and olive salsa 110
Kofta burgers with mango-sweet chilli sauce 14
Coffee ice cream bombes with crushed raspberries and macadamia nut wafers 106

Chilled pea and lettuce soup with crispy ham 12
Spice-rubbed spatchcock chicken with Greek-style salad 16
Cracked paprika potatoes 105
Mango and granadilla queen of puddings 30

Autumn:

Creamy chicken and leek pie with polenta topping 44
Tabbouleh 23
Surprise granadilla pudding 51

Chicken pie with roasted peppers and feta 64
Broccoli with lemon breadcrumbs 56
White chocolate meringues with kiwi fruit 69

Winter:

Bruschetta with herbed cream cheese and smoked snoek 101
Venison pie 58
Panna cotta with lavender biscuits and orange-caramel sauce 96

Moroccan lamb and vegetable soup with chickpeas, lentils and noodles 54
Moroccan-style chicken phyllo pie 45
Spicy pear and macadamia nut crumble 50

Spring:

Caramelised onion, asparagus and gruyère tartlets 78
Marmalade-baked pork chops with kumquats and parsley rice 87
Ice cream cake with coffee fudge sauce 93

Parsley-crusted fish with cherry tomatoes, asparagus and lemon salsa verde 88
Spring onion mashed potato 83
Rustic pear and chocolate tart 70

Index

Page numbers in **bold** indicate photographs.

B

beef dishes
  burgers with mango-sweet chilli sauce, kofta 14, **15**
  fillet with asparagus, balsamic onions and chimichurri sauce, roast **100**, 104-105
  meatballs with roasted tomato and pepper sauce, Italian 66-67, **67**
  picadillo 122
    empanadas 112
    shepherd's pie with parsley potato topping 63
  steak sandwiches with grilled onion and garlic and herb butter 82
biscuits
  lavender 96
  strawberry macaroons 113
bread, mango with crunchy brown sugar topping 22

C

cakes
  ice cream with coffee fudge sauce 93
  pear and pecan nut with cream cheese frosting 46, **47**
  pecan meringue with mango and granadilla curd 26
chicken dishes
  bake, mustard chicken and vegetable 90
  Mediterranean, quick 91
  pie
    creamy chicken and leek with polenta crust 44
    Moroccan-style phyllo 45
    with roasted peppers and feta 64, **65**
  spatchcock with Greek-style salad, spice-rubbed 16-17, **17**
  spicy chicken 123
  thighs wrapped in bacon with pesto sauce, stuffed **100**, 102
  wings with tzatziki, dragon 80, **81**
compote, mango and litchi 28
curd, mango and granadilla 30
curry, Thai vegetable with peanuts and lemony jasmine rice 62

D

desserts
  apricots in rosemary syrup with pistachio nuts and Greek yoghurt 27
  Catalan cream with mango and litchi compote 28, **29**
  chocolate pots with strawberries and almond praline 94, **95**
  coffee ice cream bombes with crushed raspberries and macadamia nut wafers 106-107
  fudge tartlets with chocolate and hazelnut topping 114-115
  grape and almond tartlets 48-49, **49**
  ice cream cake with coffee fudge sauce 93
  individual malva puddings with candied citrus rind 72-73, **73**
  mango and granadilla queen of puddings 30-31, **31**
  mango bread with crunchy brown sugar topping 22
  panna cotta with lavender biscuits and orange-caramel sauce 96-97, **97**
  pear and pecan nut cake with cream cheese frosting 46, **47**
  pecan meringue cake with mango and granadilla curd 26
  rustic pear and chocolate tart 70, **71**
  spicy pear and macadamia nut crumble 50
  strawberry macaroons 113
  surprise granadilla pudding 51
  white chocolate meringues with kiwi fruit 69
  white chocolate-chilli ice cream with caramelised nectarines 125
dough, pizza 35
dressings
  basil 24
  cherry and watercress salad 18
  mint 20

F

fish dishes
  bruschetta with herbed cream cheese and smoked snoek 101
  parsley-crusted fish with cherry tomatoes, asparagus and lemon salsa verde 88, **89**
  salmon cheesecake 103
  smoked salmon and trout phyllo tartlets **108**, 109
  tuna and avocado melts 56, **57**

I

ice cream 106, 125

L

lamb dishes
  soup, Moroccan lamb and vegetable with chickpeas, lentils and noodles 54
  tagine with prunes and almonds 60, **61**
lemons, preserved 34
light meals
  bruschetta
    with goat's cheese and pepper and olive salsa **108**, 110
    with herbed cream cheese and smoked snoek 101
  cakes, cheesy ham and potato with avocado 38, **38**
  dates and oranges with Greek yoghurt and toasted sunflower seeds **116**, 117
  frittata, broccoli and feta 119
  muffins
    bacon and asparagus 76, **77**
    mini toad-in-the-hole 111
  panini, mushroom, blue cheese and peppadew™ 84, **85**
  picadillo empanadas 112
  pizza with crisp smoked ham and avocado 35
  puffs, cheesy pesto 110, **108**
  salmon cheesecake 103
  sandwiches
    pan-fried mozzarella and salami 34
    steak with grilled onion and garlic and herb butter 82
  sausages with onion marmalade, bacon-wrapped **116**, 118

tart, baby marrow and ricotta cheese 92
tartlets
caramelised onion, asparagus and Gruyère 78-79
roasted pepper, olive and feta 36-37, **37**
smoked salmon and trout phyllo **108**, 109
tuna and avocado melts 56, **57**
wings with tzatziki, dragon 80, **81**

M
muffins
bacon and asparagus 76, **77**
mini toad-in-the-hole 111

P
pasta, spaghetti carbonara with rocket 39
pastry 36, 70, 78
almond 48
shortcrust
rich 58
sweet 114
pies
chicken
and leek with polenta crust, creamy 44
Moroccan-style phyllo 45
with roasted peppers and feta 64, **65**
picadillo shepherd's with parsley potato topping 63
venison 58-59
pork dishes
chops, marmalade-baked with kumquats and parsley rice 87
fillet with caramelised onions and plums 42, **43**
fillet kebabs with dried apricot couscous 19

R
rub, spice 16

S
salads
brown and wild rice with mango, pecan nuts and mint 23
cherry and watercress with warm goat's cheese 18
Greek-style 16
mixed pepper, dried fig and pine nut 24, **25**
roasted butternut with pecan nuts and feta 63
rocket, spanspek and Black Forest ham with mint dressing 20, **21**
sandwiches
mozzarella and salami, pan-fried 34
steak with grilled onion and garlic and herb butter 82
sauces, savoury
chimichurri 104
lemon salsa verde 88
mango-sweet chilli 14
pesto sauce 102
roasted tomato and pepper 66
salsa
fresh corn and avocado 124
roasted pepper and olive 124
sun-dried tomato pesto 102
sauces, sweet
coffee fudge 93
malva pudding 72
orange-caramel 96
whisky-custard 50
side dishes and accompaniments
asparagus **100**, 104
broccoli with lemon breadcrumbs 56
cherry tomatoes, roasted 117
dried apricot couscous 19
lemons, preserved 34
mushroom ragout 40, **41**
onions, balsamic **100**, 104
polenta
crisp wedges 40, **41**
pancakes **120**, 123
soft, with leeks 68
potatoes
cracked paprika **100**, 105
spring onion mashed 83
rice
lemony jasmine 62
parsley 87
risotto primavera 86
tabbouleh with preserved lemon 23
tzatziki 80
Welsh rarebit toast 55
soups
chilled pea and lettuce with crispy ham 12, **13**
chunky cauliflower with Welsh rarebit toast 55
Moroccan lamb and vegetable with chickpeas, lentils and noodles 54
tortilla 121

T
tarts and tartlets
baby marrow and ricotta cheese 92
rustic pear and chocolate 70, **71**
caramelised onion, asparagus and Gruyère 78-79
fudge with chocolate and hazelnut topping 114-115
grape and almond 48-49, **49**
roasted pepper, olive and feta 36-37, **37**
smoked salmon and trout phyllo **108**, 109
toppings, savoury
onion marmalade 118
pizza 35
polenta 44
toppings, sweet
almond praline 94
candied citrus rind 72
caramelised nectarines 125
chocolate and hazelnut 115
cream cheese frosting 46
fudge 114
macadamia nut crumble 50
meringue 30

V
vegetarian main dishes
baby marrow and ricotta cheese tart 92
mushroom ragout with crisp polenta wedges 40, **41**
risotto primavera 86
Thai vegetable curry with peanuts and lemony jasmine rice 62
venison, pie 58-59

W
wafers, macadamia nut 106